# POLLUTION ABATEMENT

# POLLUTION ABATEMENT

*Edited by* K M Clayton & R C Chilver

**DAVID & CHARLES** : **NEWTON ABBOT**

0 7153 6128 7

Set in 11/13 IBM Press Roman
and printed in Great Britain by W J Holman  Dawlish  Devon
for David & Charles (Holdings) Limited
South Devon House  Newton Abbot  Devon

# Contents

# List of Diagrams

# Preface

This is an edited record of a seminar held at the University of East Anglia in October 1971. It was one of a series organised by Professor Lord Zuckerman, with financial support from the Ford Foundation, designed to bring together those in government, industry and the universities who are concerned with environmental problems.

It followed an exploratory one-day conference on the same problems held at the same university in July 1971, which helped to prepare for the seminar in October. One or two of the contributions here are based on material delivered in July.

The following took part in the seminar:

*Chairman:* Professor Lord Zuckerman, OM, KCB
R. Arculus, Head of the Science and Technology Department, Foreign and Commonwealth Office
Dr H. H. Atkinson, Senior Principal Scientific Officer, Cabinet Office
Julian Ash, Graduate Student, School of Environmental Sciences
Professor W. Beckerman, Head of the Department of Political Economy, University College, London
J. Bullock, Planning Department, Norfolk County Council
Monsieur M. Carpentier, Commission de Communautés Européennes, Brussels

A. Cartwright, Head of the Geography Department, Keswick Hall
    College of Education
R. C. Chilver, CB, Deputy Secretary, Department of the
    Environment
Prof K. M. Clayton, Pro-Vice-Chancellor, School of Environmental
    Sciences, University of East Anglia
Dr B. G. Clarke, Lecturer, School of Environmental Sciences,
    University of East Anglia
Professor H. A. Cole, Director of the Fisheries Laboratory,
    Lowestoft
Professor D. D. Davies, Dean of the School of Biological Sciences,
    University of East Anglia
Professor A. R. Emerson, Professor of Sociology, School of Social
    Studies, University of East Anglia
M. L. O. Faber, Alternate Director, Overseas Development Group,
    University of East Anglia
Professor B. M. Funnell, Professor of Environmental Sciences and Dean,
    School of Environmental Sciences, University of East
    Anglia
Sir George Godber, KCB, DM, Chief Medical Officer, Department
    of Health and Social Security
Dr M. George, Regional Officer, Nature Conservancy, Norwich
I. J. Gillespie, Lecturer, Overseas Development Group, University
    of East Anglia
Professor M. B. Glauert, Professor of Mathematics, School of
    Mathematics and Physics, University of East Anglia
Professor J. Gottman, School of Geography, University of Oxford
Dr J. G. Harvey, Lecturer, School of Environmental Sciences,
    University of East Anglia
Dr R. Haynes, Lecturer, School of Environmental Sciences,
    University of East Anglia
Professor T. P. Hill, Professor of Economics and Dean of the
    School of Social Studies, University of East Anglia
Dr M. W. Holdgate, Department of the Environment, Central Unit

on the Environment

M. Hutchings, Graduate Student, School of Environmental
 Sciences, University of East Anglia

N. A. Iliff, Member of the Royal Commission on Environmental
 Pollution

F. E. Ireland, Chief Alkali Inspector, Department of the
 Environment

Dr R. L. Jeffries, Lecturer, School of Biological Sciences,
 University of East Anglia

Dr R. A. Y. Jones, Senior Lecturer, School of Chemical Sciences,
 University of East Anglia

J. F. T. Langley, Chairman, Confederation of British Industry,
 Environmental & Technical Legislation Committee

Professor P. J. Lawther, Director, MRC Air Pollution Unit, St
 Bartholomew's Hospital Medical College

A. J. Lippitt, Assistant Secretary, Industrial and Commercial
 Policy Division, Department of Trade and Industry

Dr P. S. Liss, Lecturer, School of Environmental Sciences,
 University of East Anglia

Dr G. J. MacDonald, Council on Environmental Quality,
 Washington DC, USA

Professor A. S. Mackintosh, Director, Overseas Development
 Group, University of East Anglia

Dr C. F. Mason, Senior Research Associate, School of Biological
 Sciences, University of East Anglia

Dr E. E. Pochin, CBE, Director, MRC Department of Clinical Research,
 University College Hospital Medical School

B. T. Price, Director of Planning Development, Vickers Ltd

Dr D. S. Ranwell, Director, Coastal Ecology Research Station,
 Norwich

Dr A. J. Robinson, Director, Warren Springs Laboratory, Stevenage

Dr M. E. C. Sant, Director, Leverhulme Project, Centre of East
 Anglian Studies, University of East Anglia

D. Serwer, Research Associate, United National Institute for

Training and Research, New York
Professor N. Sheppard, FRS, Professor of Chemical Sciences,
      School of Chemical Sciences, University of East Anglia
P. Slater, Graduate student, School of Environmental Sciences,
      University of East Anglia
Dr J. R. Tarrant, Lecturer, School of Environmental Sciences,
      University of East Anglia
Dr A. Young, Reader, School of Environmental Sciences, University of East Anglia

Mr Serwer and M. Carpentier described the policies and activities of the institutions to which they belong. Other members of the seminar spoke for themselves, though basing their remarks on their experience or studies in environmental administration or research.

# 1: Fundamentals

The first paper in this chapter is an analysis by Dr Holdgate of the concepts that are used in the control of pollution, namely the 'target' or 'receptor' exposed to risk of pollution, the size of the effect of the pollution, the risk of a specified effect occurring, and criterion, which is the probability of an effect of a specified size on a specified target. From criteria standards are evolved, which can be divided into 'primary standards' and 'derived working levels'. Dr Holdgate discusses how these factors are evaluated and the uses to which they are put. His paper is followed by an account by Dr Gordon MacDonald of the philosophy and practices that are being developed in the United States. Mr Langley then discusses the implications for industry of the various ways in which standards are evolved and applied, and the relationship that should exist between government and industry in evolving and applying them.


**THE BASIS FOR STANDARDS**  *M. W. Holdgate* *
A pollutant can most conveniently be defined as something that is in the wrong place at the wrong time and in the wrong quantity. By its very lack of scientific precision this definition emphasises two things: first, that the seriousness of pollution depends on the context, and second that the acceptability of pollution − the degree to which it is 'wrong' − depends on value judgements that

* For an Appendix to this paper see page 198                    *15*

inevitably vary with environmental, social and economic circumstances.

Pollutants are important in proportion to their effects. In assessing the seriousness of such effects one inevitably considers:

   1  the *target* — the organism or resource to be protected from the pollutant — and its value to society;
   2  the *magnitude of the effect*, both in spatial extent and in its degree of severity on individual target organisms or resources.

The ranking of targets is arbitrary. It usually starts with man, turning next to domestic livestock and crops, and then to structures liable to corrosion, to wild life, and finally to amenity. This traditional ranking order may well prove not to be the wisest when knowledge is more complete. For example, it is important to protect the stability of the basic systems on which the renewal of atmospheric oxygen depends, and for this reason the plankton of our oceans, if at risk, could well be a target of higher importance even than man.

It is important in analysing the conceptual basis for 'standards' to note two fundamental terms — 'risk' and 'criteria'. Risk is the probability of an adverse effect of defined size and kind on a target in a defined period. To calculate a risk, of course, one has to specify what is to be considered the 'undesirable effect' in the particular context, and this can range from death through a whole series of clinical and sub-clinical symptoms, to such minutiae as the minor derangement of haemoglobin synthesis at low concentrations of lead in the blood, or the minor disturbance of fish behaviour at very low levels of DDT in fresh water. Social judgements, often of an arbitrary kind, colour this judgement of what constitutes an undesirable effect. Generally human death is unacceptable as a consequence of pollution, and this means that one must be concerned with protecting those individuals in the population who are most at risk. But this may not be so when dealing with populations of other organisms when one may well accept a small death-roll.

One must also balance one effect against another, and the costs of
amelioration in each case. In certain developing countries, basic
environmental hygiene measures could add ten years to the expec-
tation of life, and such improvement has higher priority than a
change in pollution that may prolong one or two lives by one or two
years. The important thing is that there are almost infinite gradua-
tions in what constitutes an unacceptable risk for human societies
over the world, and this obviously has implications when one
comes to regulatory protective measures in which standards and
other actions are involved. We must not expect global uniformity
in the value judgements of such widely different societies as we
have at the present time.

In assessing risk, one must be concerned with the *total* body
intake in man, or *total* impact from all sources, of a particular
pollutant. Care must be taken not to get sidetracked into over-
concern with general environmental risks and under-concern with
risks at work or in the home, for all must be evaluated equally.
Lead provides a good example of this. People have recently laid
great stress on possible risks from airborne lead, but have given less
emphasis to the much larger quantities of lead which pass through
our system in our food and drinking water. Even less do they note
that old lead paint in sub-standard houses remains the commonest
cause of lead poisoning in children. Yet it is the total amount from
all sources that matters.

A 'risk' thus defined is a point on a continuous curve relating
concentration of a pollutant to a target: effects will vary with
individual target organisms within a species according to the health,
nutritional state or environmental circumstances of the target, and
also because the 'threshold' above which pollutants produce a particular effect may differ according to whether they are acting alone
or with others. This is the meaning of the stress on 'environmental
variable, and, target variables' in the definition. (See also page 198)

Nonetheless, in principle, these relationships are capable of rigorous scientific definition. In practice we have, in many cases, bad

and inadequate curves, and often we have not chosen wisely what
to measure, or how to measure it. However possible it may be to
define criteria in theory: in a real world one has limited technique
and limited resources and must make value judgements about
priorities for study and probabilities in interpretation. There are
very few pollutants about which we really know enough. In science
stress is often laid on the need for a 'null hypothesis' susceptible to
experimental test. There are two such as regards pollution: 'substance "X" is harmless', in which case experiments can be designed
to test for the most likely harmful effects; and 'substance "X" is
likely to be toxic and should be assumed guilty', in which
case experiments are designed to determine its innocence. Both
courses converge, but it seems to me that where there is an established pattern of use in industry, investment, legislation or regulation,
governments tend to assume that a newly-accused pollutant is
innocent unless proved guilty, whereas, from an academic stand-
point, it is often tempting to take the second hypothesis that,
since the thing can be toxic, it should be subject to regulatory
measures until proved harmless.

'Standards' are set on the basis of such evaluations in order to
prevent an unacceptable risk: they form part of a regulatory process. It follows that they inevitably depend on a value judgement.
There are two basic kinds of standard:

1 *Primary standards*, defining maximal acceptable levels of
pollutant in the target or some part of it, or the maximal
acceptable rate of intake by the target.
2 *Derived working levels* or *limits* which are devices to ensure
that the target is not exposed to environmental concentrations
of a pollutant which might lead to unacceptable risk.

Only a few primary standards have so far been set. They are
commonest in the radiation field, but include maximal allowable
levels of organochlorines and heavy metals in human tissues, and
maximal allowable intake of such materials by man. It may be
possible to extend the list somewhat; for example, to take in

primary standards for domestic livestock and, in man, for benz-
pyrenes and other known carcinogens. For the most part, however,
protection of target organisms or resources will demand action at
a preceding stage in the chain of interactions culminating in risk —
and this preceding section will commonly involve establishment of
a derived working level.

Such derived working levels include most 'standards' in common
use. They include maximal allowable concentrations in an area of
environment, the maximal allowable concentration in an emission
to the environment, the maximal allowable concentration of something in a product, or a code of practice. A technical group assem-
bled by the Preparatory Committee for the Stockholm Conference
on the Human Environment gave thought to the application of
such standards. They believed that, in choosing the kind of derived
working level to apply, one must be guided by efficiency, practica-
bility and expediency and not be ashamed of it because the objective is simply the protection of the target, and one must use the
best practical means to that end. If one is seeking environmental
quality standards, for example, it is very much easier to specify
the maximal allowable concentration of a pollutant in a defined
body of the environment not subject to gross mixing and dilution.
Conversely, the curve relating emissions at various scattered points
to subsequent concentration after mixing and dilution in a turbulent airstream is very difficult to determine. It may be almost
impossible under the latter conditions to work back from some
notional maximal allowable concentration of say $SO_2$ in the air to
the limits that actually have to be imposed on emissions in order
not to exceed that level. If that is so, it may be very much better
not to set a notional standard that is of little use, but to go directly to reducing the emissions and monitor the results to see whether
exposures have been reduced to an acceptable degree or not.

One conclusion — and this is logically inescapable when one
recognises the lack of scientific knowledge about criteria
(especially exposure/effect relationships) is that any derived

working levels, whether environmental quality standards or emission standards, will require progressive revision as knowledge improves, and should not be 'fossilised' by incorporation in inflexible regulations or treated as if they had some absolute and unchanging validity.

A second conclusion is, that, because such standards are set in order to prevent a target being put at unacceptable risk by excessive exposure, they must be expected to vary from one country to another according to environmental and social circumstances, one affecting the dispersal, and hence concentration, of the pollutant and the exposure of the target, and the other determining what is regarded as 'acceptable'. Thirdly, in view of the inevitable inaccuracy of most standards, based as they are on little more than 'guesstimates', it is wise, as the technical group recognised, to keep the level of a pollutant in an emission as low as is practicable taking social and economic factors into account. In essence this amounts to endorsement of the 'best practicable means' approach which has two advantages: it demands continued effort at pollution control so far as technology allows; and it recognises that this effort must be kept in balance with other demands on the resources of the community.

At present the overwhelming need is to improve our knowledge of criteria. The scientific literature abounds with examples where the need for regulatory action is in dispute because of uncertainties over dose/response relationships. Such examples include mercury in fish, lead and sulphur dioxide in the atmosphere, and DDT in fresh water and the sea. Not only is the relationship between the concentration of such materials in the environment and the effect on target organisms or resources imperfectly known, but there are further uncertainties over the relationship between the concentrations of pollutants in discharge to the environment and the concentrations subsequently attained in various places. This is well illustrated by the debate over the degree to which forests and lakes in Scandinavia are affected by sulphur oxides emitted in other

European countries, and over the relative importance of curbing emission in Sweden itself, or in more distant areas if these effects are to be prevented.

Such rigorous scientific criteria have both an 'offensive' and a 'defensive' value. Offensively, because they may prove a need for a redistribution of priorities for pollution control. Defensively, because eloquent individuals and pressure groups often exaggerate the importance of some pollutant against which they urge action. Scientific rigour is most important as a basis for the community's choices.

The technical group I have mentioned rightly stressed that international agreement can, and should, be sought on criteria, for these are scientific and, provided compatible methods are used with due competence, should have universal validity. The international scientific literature, specialist symposia, work of non-governmental bodies such as ICSU, and of intergovernmental organisations such as WHO or WMO, all provide means for the interchange of this basic information. The United Nations Specialised Agencies in particular have a role in convening experts (including government representatives) to discuss how far formal international recognition can be given to data on pollutant effects. These agencies, and especially WHO, are also well placed to consider where new primary protection standards are appropriate. Equally, the establishment of derived working limits and action levels must largely be a matter for national authorities, and because it calls for the interpretation of the basic scientific criteria in accordance with national environmental, economic, administrative and social circumstances, cannot be expected to lead naturally to the same pattern of derived working limits in all countries, or even all parts of the same large country. Such divergences are a matter of common observation today. For example, the United States and Canada have 'action levels' for mercury in fish of 0.5 parts per million: in Japan and Sweden the level is 1 part per million; and no other country has formalised such a limit. In Britain the control of air pollution from major industries is based on emission control on a 'best practicable means' principle, and environmental quality standards in terms of maximal allowable concentrations of pollutants in air have not been found useful other than as general guidelines or goals. In other countries environmental quality standards have been adopted as a major element in pollution control policies. Such difference are to be expected, and the whole logic of the situation demands freedom for governments to adopt the machinery that, in each case, best helps them to attain the degree of pollution control they desire.

It is very welcome that the Preparatory Committee should have endorsed the concept of 'best practicable means' — ie the concept that the level of pollutant should be kept as low as is practicable, taking economic, social and technical factors into account. However desirable it may be to set environmental quality standards, emission standards, or other derived working limits, doing so does not excuse industries and authorities from doing the best they can to minimise discharges of known hazardous substances into the environment. Of course, there is a need for balance here. London smoke has been reduced to the level where it is no longer a serious hazard, and while opportunities to reduce it further may be worth taking, it is clearly better to use our limited resources to clean up the areas that remain 'black' and smoky.

Uniform international standards may be urged for two reasons. One is that making pollution control uniformly strict in adjacent or economically linked countries is necessary to satisfy public opinion or to equalise the burden on industry amd avoid giving an 'unfair' competitive advantage to an industry subject to less stringent controls. The other is that non-tariff barriers should bot be erected against trade. As to the first, pollution control can be made equally effective in different countries without an identical system of standards, and it is better to leave communities free to attain goals of environmental quality using the methods best suited to their circumstances. The second argument is valid, but it needs to be

applied carefully. For example, every time a citizen of the Canadian
plains is forced to buy a car that complies with standards of exhaust
emission, set because of the pollution problems in major cities
in the United States, about £80 is spent needlessly.


## A UNITED STATES VIEW  *G. MacDonald*
There are three main ways of controlling industrial pollution, and
the United States aims to use all three. The first way is persuasion,
which may work at times, but has not proved as effective as one
might hope. The second is setting standards and enforcing them
through legal constraints. The third is applying user charges or
economic incentives of one kind or another.

I will start with the problems of setting standards and enforcing
them. I would agree that by themselves, standards do not deal
effectively with all pollution problems. In some cases they are
clearly needed; for example, in dealing with toxic materials. At
the same time we must recognise that prohibiting absolutely the
disposal of materials to the environment is as unwarranted as
allowing unlimited freedom to do so. Technical and economic
feasibility need to be considered. There are difficulties of enforcement, and public opposition is created when enforcement leads to
unemployment. In the United States standards have sometimes
proved so onerous that they have not been enforced, which is unfair to those who are trying to comply with them. Enforcing them
sometimes works out inequitably. Complying with a standard for
effluents may cost a small firm proportionately five times as much
as a large one; though it is the large firm's effluent that has most
effect on the environment. We believe that, in the long term, the
charge system can deal efficiently, effectively and equitably with
the problem of pollution. I hope to describe later how this is being
approached in the United States.

Perhaps I can describe now the mechanism by which standards
are set, and I would like to distinguish between air, water and

chemicals because the procedures are quite different in the three areas. Radiation, a fourth area, follows along the same lines as chemicals.

Air pollution was originally considered a 'public nuisance', and so was dealt with on a local basis. The situation changed considerably as a result of the Donora incident, and federal legislation began to be passed in the middle and late fifties. Strengthening of the air pollution legislation came in 1967 with the Air Quality Act. This act provides for a system of criteria, and the federal government developed these criteria and passed them on to the states. The states attempted to achieve the recommended criteria. They were not mandatory, and under the 1967 act there was nothing labelled 'Emission Standard' or 'Ambient Air Quality Standard', but a requirement was placed on the federal government to try and achieve these criteria. The situation changed dramatically in 1970 when the president signed the Clean Air Act Amendments which provided for national ambient air standards as well as minor things dealing with cars. National air standards are achieved through a systematic process. The first step in this process is establishing air quality criteria. These are prepared by a group that includes representatives of the academic world, government and industry, who survey all the scientific evidence available at the time. Before they are issued, a detailed economic evaluation of the effects of standards based on these criteria is carried out. The point of this economic analysis is to assess the impact on the federal budget, and also on the private sector. (This kind of analysis, we feel, is particularly important considering the present state of the economy). With the help of these scientific and economic analyses, primary and secondary standards have now been established, and it is the responsibility of the states to meet the primary standards within nine months, and the secondary ones within twenty-seven months. I think it is a process that is well under way, and the states have developed a capability of carrying through this process under a system of federal grants.

The Air Pollution Control Administration published requirements for vehicle emissions in 1967 which came into force in 1970.
These requirements were largely the result of work done in the
state of California. Estimates were made of the emission standards
required in order to achieve the kind of ambient standards hoped
for in 1970-75 and 1980. Congress decided that 1980 was too far
off and moved back five years to 1975, and that was the genesis
of the requirements for the 1975 models of a ninety per-cent reduction over 1970 permitted emissions for hydrocarbons and carbon
monoxides.

Let me turn briefly to water. We are moving towards ensuring
that waters can support aquatic life and can safely be swum in by
human beings. A very similar approach will be used as with air
quality standards. Effluent limitations will be issued, and these will
be tightened as we approach the 1980 and 1985 deadlines.

Control of chemicals in the environment is a joint responsibility
between EPA and the Food and Drug Administration. Mercury and
other potentially toxic materials will now be controlled through
the EPA.

## AN INDUSTRIALIST'S VIEW *J. F. T. Langley*

*Introduction*
Industrialists, for the most part, are not scientists, nor are we
expert in anything unless it be the day-to-day running of factories.
Most of these factories are small. There are about 90,000 industrial
establishments in the United Kingdom as defined by the census of
production. It is not generally realised that, of these 90,000 establishments, no less than 76,500 employ less than 200 people. The
household names that spring to mind whenever industrial matters
are discussed are far from typical of British industry. It is true that
some of these 76,500 establishments are part of big groups and
therefore have access to the resources and specialised services which

a big group can provide, but the great majority are independent and have to rely upon their own efforts.

Those who run these factories are pretty ordinary people, and very often of no great academic brilliance. Nevertheless, they are at the centre of the wealth-creating process which is both the major cause of the problem of environmental pollution, and the best hope of its solution. They are the people who make decisions about capital expenditure, who sit on the Councils of Trade Associations, on River Authorities, and on County District and County Councils. These are people who have problems on their desks which demand immediate attention — a machine breakdown, a delivery problem, a labour dispute, a trade recession. Compared with these pressing matters a concern for the environment may not be uppermost in their minds, and yet it is these people to whom you have to get through, for all scientists and all great thinkers of the world will be whistling down the wind unless they have industry with them to translate thought into practice.

This is said, not in a spirit of arrogance, but rather of humility. To a great extent it explains why I am here. A prime function of the Environmental and Technical Legislation Committee of the Confederation of British Industry is to interpret and disseminate scientific and governmental thinking on these matters to the CBI's 11,500 members either directly, or through affiliated trade associations: equally it is our function in the reverse direction to express the views of industry to scientists and to government. In the past the CBI's role in the field of technical legislation has been a defensive one: the protection of its members from ill-considered or impractical measures. I am hopeful that we can now move to a more positive role whereby the industrialist can edge a little closer to the idealism of the environmentalist, and those primarily concerned with the environment can edge a little closer to the practical problems of the industrialist.

I remain an optimist. Nothing is as irresistible as an idea whose moment has come. An awareness of the pollution problem *has* come on a world-wide scale, and I believe that, in the next few years, great strides will be made towards its solution.

*Machinery for determining standards and standards policy*
This item on the agenda refers to the role of individual govern-ments, of industry, and of international organisations, in deter-mining standards and standards policy. Of these three it seems probable that in the next few years we shall find ourselves increas-ingly preoccupied with the international role. This is in no way to minimise the importance of the domestic scene; rather it recognises that, in the United Kingdom, reasonably effective machinery exists for the determination of standards and standards policy. Obviously there is scope for improvement and refinement, but at least we have something to build on, whereas internationally we are starting from scratch.

In the United Kingdom the responsibilities of industrial manage-ment in the prevention of pollution are largely defined by statute. There is a considerable corpus of legislation, some of it of long standing, most of it post the second world war. Common Law provides additional protection. Under Common Law the classic case is the Macnaghten judgement on the rights of riparian owners. Similar rights could no doubt be established in respect of atmos-pheric pollution or the noise nuisance. The fact that Common Law cases are comparatively rare does not alter the fact that they can be brought, and the implications of this are not lost on industry.

In the general approach towards the fixing and enforcement of standards there is virtually no difference of objective between the government and the CBI. The Confederation is fully aware of the need for industry to take an increasingly active part in matters relating to the environment. It has supported many measures to abate pollution and has worked closely with government and with the enforcement authorities. That this has been possible is thanks in no small measure to the flexible manner in which legislation has been drafted and applied; the system of consent to discharges and the principle of 'best practicable means'. The aim has been to ensure a constructive approach to these problems, and a realistic assessment of what can be achieved, and when.

To achieve this we have devised reasonably sophisticated consultative machinery. This operates through the CBI's Environmental and Technical Legislation Committee. This Committee has standing Panels on Clean Air, Synthetic Detergents, Water and Effluent, Industrial Solid Wastes, Weights and Measures, and Oil Legislation. There is also a Private Bills Panel: this scrutinises up to one hundred private bills a year, most of them sponsored by local authorities and most having some bearing on the environmental problem. After consulting the appropriate panel or industrial sector, representations are made to the sponsors of the bills in cases where amendment (hopefully, constructive amendment) seems necessary. In the great majority of cases agreement is reached at panel level. A few cases are brought to the main committee, while only a tiny minority reach the stage of a petition to parliament. The Private Bills Panel attaches much importance to − and I think has been successful in − establishing a reputation for responsibility in the sense that, if amendments are sought, they are sought on matters upon which industry feels strongly and not in a spirit of unconstructive opposition.

I think that over the past twelve months there has been a subtle change in the way the Environmental and Technical Legislation Committee operates. Previously its role was largely defensive: to wait for draft legislation to appear and then to protect the interests of CBI members where this seemed necessary. I believe we are now moving to a more positive role. We have, for instance, greatly strengthened our contacts with government. We sometimes find ourselves a little puzzled to know which department deals with what, but it would be churlish to complain too much about this as some overlapping is inevitable, and the position has been much simplified by the amalgamation of several ministries in the

Department of the Environment. Incidentally we regard this as a
great step forward which should enable coherent policies to be
worked out over a wide field. It is a bit early to say how this huge
department will work in practice, but we think the signs are
encouraging. It is also our wish to associate ourselves closely with
the work of Sir Eric Ashby's Royal Commission.

In pursuit of the more positive role to which I have referred, we
have told government that we hold ourselves in readiness to provide
expert support for United Kingdom delegations to international
meetings on environmental matters. We have also established a
policy panel which can express an opinion on policy matters relating to the whole field of the environment rather than to specific
sectors. In this way it will be our aim to ensure that the United
Kingdom view is heard clearly in international circles. An example
is the vexed question of international standards on which the
United Kingdom has views to which I refer in a later chapter.

In talking of the CBI Committee's activities and aims I am conscious of the danger of giving the impression that everything is
perfect. This would be far from the truth, but at least we have
some machinery in existence for determining standards, and we
have probably gone further down the road on a consultative, flexible, semi-voluntary basis than certain other countries whose
approach has been more rigid.

If I may turn to the role of government for a moment, there are
ways in which they can help, not so much in determining standards,
but in creating a climate in which the right standards can be determined.

Firstly government has an educational role. There is a rather
dangerous catch-phrase in current use to the effect that the polluter
must pay the cost of eliminating his pollution. This can obscure the
fact that, in the final analysis, it is society who must pay either
through higher rates, higher prices, or higher taxes. I am not in
favour of too much 'gloom and doom', but I think the public
should be educated to understand that there must be built into the

cost of an article an element of environmental preservation, just as
there is now built into the cost of an article an element for safe
working conditions, pensions for the employees, and so on. In
order to bring about this process of education a little bit of 'gloom
and doom' may be necessary, but if it is overdone it will defeat the
object. Perhaps this is the moment to mention Edward Goldsmith's
concluding chapter of the book *Can Britain Survive?* This is pro-
foundly pessimistic. If it causes us a good deal of soul searching
and helps us to face up to things we should prefer to brush under
the carpet, well and good; if it induces a sense of fatalism and des-
pair, this is less good. My belief is that it takes too little account of
human ingenuity and adaptability.

Secondly, government must do more to set an example. Some of
us in private industry are inclined to get restive when we see the
waste of desolation left by mining operations or railway closures,
or hear of the substandard effluent discharged by many public
authorities. That some of this is a legacy from private enterprises
is not denied, but the industries to which I have referred have been
nationalised for a generation and their record of conservation is
not impressive. Lest it should be said that in these cases public
money is involved, I would counter that, in contrast to private
industry, I cannot recall any case of a nationalised industry or a
local authority being allowed to go bankrupt. From the point of
view of CBI members, the Latin tag *'Quis custodiet ipsos custodes'*
is rather apt.

Thirdly, on the subject of government's role, we are terribly
short of knowledge of what pollution actually costs. If industry,
acting on behalf of the community, decides on economic grounds
not to install plant to abate pollution, the apparent savings are
almost certainly illusory, since the community will incur the cost
in other currency, perhaps in shorter plant life, higher cleaning
costs, higher labour absenteeism. If some attempt could be made
to quantify what has been described as the 'delayed economic costs'
it would help in a fourth area where government should be active:

the determination of priorities. I question whether we have got this right. A great deal of energy is devoted to hypothetical problems half a century hence rather than to cures for existing environmental evils. By all means let us keep an eye on the next century, but let us keep it in perspective. As the *Financial Times* put it recently, we seem greatly concerned that sonic booms may shatter stained glass, but less concerned that many superb churches and other ancient monuments are ringed with derelict property. In this connection government must do more through planning procedures, either local or national, to check the spread of urban sprawl which is the cause of so much environmental evil.

In conclusion, I wonder whether it might not be possible to enlist the idealism of youth in the cause of the environment? Some of us regretted the passing of National Service, not from a jingoistic point of view, but because it fostered the idea of service. Voluntary Service Overseas has been successful in a limited way. If the reintroduction of compulsory National Service for the Environment is politically impossible, it might be possible to introduce Voluntary Service for the Environment, through which young people might help to clean up some of the eyesores which defile the country.


## DISCUSSION

A brief discussion showed general agreement with the analysis in these three contributions of the various intellectual tools used by government in framing practical means of controlling pollution and of the forms that these practical means can take. In particular, there was no disposition to question the opinion that definition of a desired result in terms of environmental quality is not by itself a useful basis legally or administratively and of doubtful value as an aid towards framing practical measures of control.

# 2: The Scientific Input

This chapter consists of five papers illustrating, in typical fields of knowledge bearing on control of pollution, the scientific information available to governments; the present limitations of this information; and the research needed to improve it. The subjects and authors are:

| | |
|---|---|
| Hazards from radiation | Dr Pochin |
| Air pollution and its effects on man | Professor Lawther |
| Measurement of atmospheric pollution | Dr Davies |
| The behaviour of $SO_2$ and other gases in crossing an air-water interface | Dr Liss |
| Suspended matter in estuaries and coastal waters | Dr Liss |

**HAZARDS FROM RADIATION** *E. E. Pochin*
In many ways a discussion of radiation protection procedures gives a valuable starting point for the more general review of the types of control and precaution that should be appropriate in the case of

*32*

other forms of environmental contaminant. Ionising radiation has
many features in common with many chemical and some physical
pollutants. Exposure to radiation may occur in the working
environment, involving also, to some extent, the general population, and special sections of it selectively. It is quantitatively
measurable, and at certain levels produces various damaging effects
in human beings. Some of these effects occur soon or immediately
after exposure, if doses are high. Others only occur after long lat-
ency and may follow lower doses; and similar mutagenic or carcinogenic effects have also been shown to follow exposure to other
contaminants, for which the long term effects may thus prove to
be more limiting than any acute effects which are observed at the
time of exposure. In many ways, therefore, the study of ionising
radiation and criteria of protection against undue exposure have
much in common with the problems raised by other environmental
pollutants, and may offer a useful model for their control.

On the other hand, however, the harmful effects, and within
limits the environmental importance of radiation, have been widely
recognised and closely studied for many decades, markedly unlike
those of most other environmental contaminants. Sources of radiation and naturally radioactive materials were being used by 1896,
and their damaging effects in man were recognised soon after this,
in some cases within a few years. Since then there has been extensive research into radiobiological effects — some people would say
disproportionately much — and a valuable structure has been developed for advice, protection recommendations, and, the most
difficult job of all, the attempted quantitative estimation of
hazard. The international basis for the review of radiation levels
and protection criteria is outlined in the appendix (page 36), and
it is not necessary to discuss this in detail here. Certain aspects
should however be emphasised in order to open the discussion of
comparable methods that should be applicable to other environmental pollutants.

Firstly, it is apparent already that it has been possible to set up useable quantitative criteria for the adequately safe control of a wide range of types of occupational exposure to radiation. The current health statistics of occupations involving exposure to radiation appear to be excellent, with the one major exception of uranium mining, in which technical and other difficulties have prevented the recommended protection criteria from being attained. The previously increased incidence of radiation-induced disease in radiologists is not now detectable, and the radium contamination of luminisers has long been recognised as hazardous and controlled. The similar importance of an increasing number of toxic chemical substances in the working environment is being identified. As for radiation, a suitable quantitative limit needs to be set in every such case to ensure that the conditions of exposure are adequately safe.

Here, the words 'adequately safe' are important. If it can be shown, or can be held, that for a particular pollutant no harm of any kind will occur unless the level of the pollutant exceeds a certain value, exposure at levels below this value will be safe in the absolute sense. If this cannot be shown, and if even the lowest exposure may involve some, perhaps correspondingly low, frequency of harm, and if some exposure is unavoidable, then a decision must be made as to the frequency of harm that could be regarded as acceptable, but which should not be exceeded, under the conditions necessitating the exposure. This is an exceedingly important point to discuss, and arises later in our programme, under the telling title 'How safe is safe?' This is not so much a technical or purely scientific problem as a question for public assessment and comment, even though the evaluation of the amount and kind of risk for any given exposure limit is a scientific one. And it is one which will arise, not only for radiation, but for any environmental contaminant for which low concentrations may occasionally give rise to harmful effects.

A feature of radiation injury which is likely to apply also to the effects of many other contaminants is that, in general, the diseases which may be produced do not differ detectably from comparable

conditions which occur naturally. This, of course, adds greatly to
the difficulty of estimating the frequency with which harmful
effects are produced in man by a given exposure. Even if a human
population has been exposed to a known dose and is then surveyed
for the induction of harmful effects, the problem will be the difficult statistical one of estimating an increase in frequency of a
naturally occurring condition. The detection of small increases
may be impossible, even if large populations can be fully studied
for the necessary long periods after exposure, and the likely effects
of small doses may need to be inferred from the measurable effects
of larger exposures.

In the case of ionising radiation, large numbers of people have
been necessarily exposed to radiation in the course of medical
treatment, and any increased occurrence of subsequent disease has
been examined in relation to the exposure to radiation of the
various tissues concerned. Similar studies of disease, and particularly of cancer and leukaemia, have been made in the populations
of the Japanese cities exposed to radiation from nuclear weapons,
in uranium and other miners liable to inhalation of radon, and in
luminisers who have accidentally ingested radium in the course of
their work. Such epidemiological studies have yielded quantitative
estimates for a number of human tissues, of the frequency of
tumours to be expected following relatively high exposures. And
inferences of at least the maximum likely frequencies can then be
made for the much lower exposures involved in permissible limits.

For other environmental contaminants it is most unlikely, and
most undesirable, that similar large scale evidence will become
available of the frequency of human injury, even from high exposures. Here the difficulties will be considerable in estimating safe,
or appropriately safe, limits on any adequate numerical basis; and
the number of new substances being introduced each year add
greatly to the difficulties involved, even if reliance is placed on
indirect estimates of human toxicity. The comparable procedure
of testing new drugs before clinical use, is, however, established

practice, and has increased in reliability with the formation of
bodies reviewing the evidence for the safety of new preparations
and the dosage in which they can be given.

I believe that our discussion can usefully be based upon considerations arising in radiation protection, and should review procedures for testing not only the immediate but also the long-term
biological effects of pollutants, including particularly mutagenic or
carcinogenic effects; the techniques of assessing numerically the
safety of particular levels and patterns of human exposure to such
substances; the ways in which a society decides, or should decide,
the degree of safety essential to any circumstances of necessary
exposure; and the structure of efficient national and international
bodies to act as authoritative sources of scientific and general advice on appropriate protection measures and·criteria for environmental pollutants.

## APPENDIX

*A note on the international basis for recommendations on
environmental pollutants*
1  It will be of considerable value to develop a source of internationally agreed recommendations with regard to potentially harmful chemical substances or physical agents that may be present in
the general or the working environment.
2  For ionising radiation, this need has been met with some success
by an International Commission on Radiological Protection (ICRP),
and by extensive research in 'radiobiology'.
3  The ICRP was set up in 1928 by the International Congress of
Radiology to advise on safety in the exposure of patients in diag-
nostic and therapeutic radiology, and of medical staff using these
procedures. With the greatly increased number of ways in which
people may be exposed to radiation and to radioactive materials,
it has extended its responsibilities to cover all forms of occupational

and population exposure. Its recommendations are very widely
adopted in the development of national regulations.

4 The Commission is non-governmental, its (thirteen) members
being 'chosen on the basis of their recognised activity in the fields of
medical radiology, radiation protection, physics, health physics,
biology, genetics, biochemistry and biophysics, with regard to an
appropriate balance of expertise rather than to nationality'. The
selection of members is made on the basis of nominations from
national delegations to the congress and from the commission
itself, and subject to approval by the International Executive
Committee of the congress. Its reports and recommendations are
published in the scientific literature directly and not through the
congress. It operates with four standing committees on different
branches of the subject, and with 'task groups' drawn largely from
outside its own membership, on particular topics requiring evaluation.

Its expenditure (about $50,000 a year, an equal sum being spent
on travelling paid for by participants' own institutions) was
largely met by the World Health Organisation (WHO) and by the
International Atomic Energy Agency (IAEA), and by the Congress
of Radiology, and was the subject of a ten-year grant by the Ford
Foundation. The commission employs a salaried staff of two
(Scientific Secretary and his secretary).

5 It does not dispose funds for research grants but influences
national programmes of research to a substantial extent. Its quantitative recommendations on 'permissible' levels of exposure to
radiation or to particular radionuclides necessarily rely on extensive national research on animal toxicity and human epidemiology.

6 Any international body set up to discharge a corresponding
function for other environmental contaminants would presumably
need to have a similar rather modest finance and staffing, but considerable authority and ability to generate the research on which
sound recommendations could be based. The optimum might be a
non-governmental body analogous to ICRP, consisting of scientists

selected for expertise rather than national distribution, if the necessary scientific base, finance, staff and authoritative position could
be created *de novo*.

7 An alternative, which might be slightly less apt but more immediately practicable, would be to use the United Nations Scientific
Committee on the Effects of Atomic Radiation (UNSCEAR) as a
model. This committee was set up by the General Assembly in
1955, essentially to evaluate fallout radiation exposures, but to do
so in the general context of all sources of radiation exposure and
estimates of their harmfulness. It is a committee of fifteen nations,
which each send delegations of one to six scientists to meetings
now occurring about annually. It has a secretariat, within the UN
Secretariat, of a Scientific Secretary, up to several scientists
seconded for periods of months to a year, and a small secretarial
staff. It reports about each two years on estimates of radiation
exposure or hazard evaluation (eg amounts of exposure from fallout, natural sources, occupation, radiology or waste disposal; and
hazard from carcinogenesis, genetic effect, injury to nervous system, impairment of immune mechanisms, etc). Its reports are made
ostensibly to the General Assembly but are immediately available
in publication (in four languages).

8 I believe that one of the useful things that UNSCEAR has done
has been to demonstrate how a subject like radiation and fallout,
involving general public significance and some emotion, can be
held under objective (and politically unanimous) scientific review,
and its reports to the General Assembly have, I think, been valuable
in this sense. It has been suggested already, by U Thant in the 1969
Committee session, that its work could form a useful model for the
approach to other environmental contaminants. It has recently
submitted an account of the basis of radiation protection procedures to the organisation of the Stockholm Conference on the
Environment; and its Scientific Secretary has been attached to the
secretariat of that conference.

9 As between a scientific committee on pollutants on the lines of

ICRP, or one parallel to UNSCEAR as a General Assembly
committee:

(a) The ICRP model is probably preferable if practicable,
since it ensures a compact group of named scientists, chosen
for their known competence in the (many) relevant fields.

(b) A United Nations committee could, however, probably
come into being more rapidly and effectively than an ICRP-
like body created *de novo*, and could have the necessary
secretariat, base, funds and some measure of 'instant authority'
from the start.


**AIR POLLUTION AND ITS EFFECTS ON MAN** *P. J. Lawther*

*Based on a discourse given to the Royal Institution on 30 October
1970, and reproduced from the Proceedings of the Royal
Institution of Great Britain by kind permission.*

On the whole, the field of radiation hazard shows some convincing
dose-response curves, and Dr Pochin is right to claim that standards
set in that field have a relatively secure basis in our knowledge of
the hazards involved. As an example of the possibility of reaching
an adequate level of understanding for well-informed decisions, the
field is an interesting one, but it is unusual among environmental
hazards. Most pollutants behave in a very complex way, and are
almost inextricably mixed up with other environmental variables.
As a result there are few simple dose-response curves, and errors of
fact and many errors in the interpretation of facts are to be found
in the literature. There is a real danger that the propagation of
some errors, especially those which lead to overstatement of the
dangers and to prophecies of doom, may eventually weaken the
obviously strong case for the prevention and abatement of pollution. In discussing air pollution, I am bound to demonstrate the
complexity of the subject, and plead for caution in the interpretation of the results of experiments. Yet this is not to deny the

welcome evidence of the beneficial effects of the Clean Air Act and
other measures which have reduced the contamination of the air we
must breathe.

A common source of confusion to those who would assess the
effect of pollution on the health of the public is the failure to
appreciate the need to distinguish between amounts of pollutants
emitted from individual sources and ground level concentrations.
The former, sometimes dramatic, estimates are often used to
frighten the public when their proper use is rather in the design of
chimneys and in town planning. The concentrations of pollutants
at ground level, or rather at lung level, are what matter in clinical
research and when this distinction is appreciated one realises that
low sources of pollution from inefficient combustion contribute
more to the fouling of the ambient air than do most industrial
chimneys; in this country the open coal fire is especially guilty –
combustion is inefficient and the smoke is discharged near the
ground.

The height of the chimney is particularly important during
temperature inversions; usually the dispersion of pollutants is
aided by the turbulence created by the rise of warm air from the
ground, but when, in calm anti-cyclonic weather, cold air under-
lies warmer layers, in effect a lid is put over a town and in these
conditions pollution from low sources may rise to alarmingly high
concentrations. Fog often accompanies this type of weather and
the admixture of smoke and fog gave rise to the hybrid term 'smog'
which meant smoke-polluted fog. The use of this term is undesirable; it is often used as if it were synonymous with air pollution
in general rather than to describe an acute form of pollution which
is chemically and physically different from the everyday variety
and may have different effects on man. This important distinction
will be discussed later.

The degree of air pollution is often reported in terms of concentration of smoke and sulphur dioxide, two of the commonest
pollutants suspected of having ill effects; smoke is produced as a

result of incomplete combustion of fuel, and sulphur-containing impurities commonly found in some fuels, especially in some coals and heavy fuel oils. Smoke and sulphur dioxide, the concentrations of which are determined on a twenty-four-hour basis in many parts of the country, are but indices of pollution which is, in fact, a highly complex mixture of many different kinds of particles floating in many gases, some of which in high concentrations are undoubtedly irritant or toxic.

The size of the particles in the air is important; particles big enough to settle out cannot penetrate far into the lung. But most of the particles present as pollutants in town air are very small, will remain airborne almost indefinitely, and can reach the alveoile of the lung. They may be seen by means of the electron microscope. Some of the particles, especially those produced by incomplete combustion, are in the form of carbonaceous aggregates and have an enormous surface area per unit mass; on these surfaces gases may be adsorbed and carried far into the lung where they may have effects quite different from those which would result from their absorption higher in the respiratory tract. Some of the particles are acidic and may, by their irritant properties, be important in producing exacerbations of respiratory or cardiac disease and may even be involved in causing chronic bronchitis. It is reasonable to believe that polluted air affects man mainly by being inhaled. The effect is not merely confined to the respiratory tract but may disturb the cardio-vascular system; soluble particles and gases may, of course, enter the blood stream, but, in general, the lungs are the primary target. The conducting airways take no part in gaseous exchange between inhaled air and the blood; they are surrounded by muscle and lined with mucus-secreting tissue and, in response to irritation or to some pharmacologically active substances, such as histamine, may be narrowed spasmodically by contractions of the surrounding muscle or by secretion of mucus in excess of normal requirements. This part of the respiratory tract is the site of asthma and bronchitis. The conducting airways lead via a transitional zone to the respiratory part of the lung, about ninety square metres in the adult, where the blood is brought very near to the inhaled air in the alveoli. These are minute sacs surrounded by capillaries through which 'venous' blood is pumped by the right ventricle of the heart. The blood, separated from the air only by the cells of the capillary membrane and the alveolar membrane, takes in oxygen and yields up the carbon dioxide produced by metabolism of the tissues. This part of the lung, to which pollutant particles may gain access if they are less than about 7 $\mu$m diameter, may be affected by pneumonia, invaded by fibrous tissue, or destroyed as in empnysema as a result of infection and chronic mechanical stress produced by airway obstruction. One must remember that destruction of the lung is inevitably accompanied by destruction of some of the blood vessels with the result that uneven perfusion and ventilation occurs and extra strain is put on the heart, since it has to work harder to pump the blood through a higher resistance. Some of these changes may occur following the inhalation of polluted air.

The most dramatic manifestation of the harmful effects of pollution is the increased mortality and morbidity which accompanies episodes of very high pollution during temperature inversions over towns. In December 1952 in London, there were at least 4,000 excess deaths attributable to the five days when pollution was very high indeed. The deaths (Fig 1) were mostly among the elderly and sick and most were due to respiratory or cardiovascular disease. The exact mechanism by which the deaths were caused is still obscure; there is no reason to believe that only one mechanisim was involved, but there are good reasons to believe that irritation, producing coughing and increase in resistance to air flow in the respiratory tract, played an important part; other more subtle effects were undoubtedly important. Increases in airways resistance would increase the work of breathing, and in diseased lungs and circulatory systems could alter ventilation/ perfusion ratios with the production of fatal disturbances in

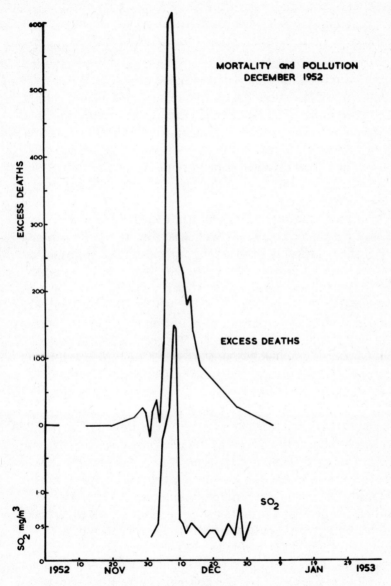

*Fig* 1    Daily deviations in deaths in Greater London (calculated
as differences from the general trend) December 1952

gaseous exchange; the increased load put on the heart could likewise prove fatal.

Variations in mortality with less dramatic changes in pollution may be seen if suitable indices are used in large enough populations. Changes in morbidity may also be studied as pollution varies from day to day. We have used deaths in Greater London and applications to the Emergency Bed Service for admission to hospital to study daily effects of pollution, as indicated by smoke and sulphur dioxide concentrations (Fig 2). Obviously the relationship between pollution and mortality will depend not only on the strength of the stress imposed but also on the susceptibility of the population exposed to the polluted air.

We 'refined' our populations by studying daily variations in the health of patients who already had chest disease. These patients, most of them suffering from severe bronchitis and emphysema, were given diaries in which they entered, by means of a simple code, their own assessment of their health day by day. The code was translated into a numerical 'score' which showed remarkably close dependence on variations of pollution measured in terms of smoke and sulphur dioxide (Fig 3). This technique has been used at intervals to assess the changing effects of pollution as it has altered over the years; the encouraging results will be shown later.

The mechanism by which polluted air causes these exacerbations may be studied clinically, by epidemiological techniques and by experimental work in the laboratory. A common clinical finding is increasing shortness of breath often accompanied by wheezing and increased production of sputum. There is an increase in resistance to air flow in the conducting airways and, as mentioned previously, this may have serious consequences if the work of breathing needed for adequate oxygenation is increased beyond tolerable limits, or if ventilation/perfusion relationships are disturbed so that  air is shunted to bloodless parts of the lung at the expense of the perfused alveoli; capillary vaso-constriction in response to low alveolar oxygen content may lead to increase in

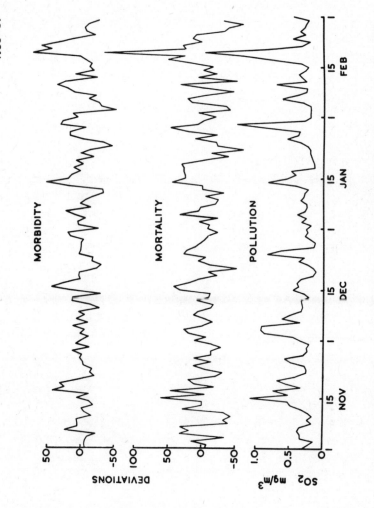

*Fig 2*   Mortality and morbidity in London, winter 1958-9: deviations from fifteen-day moving average

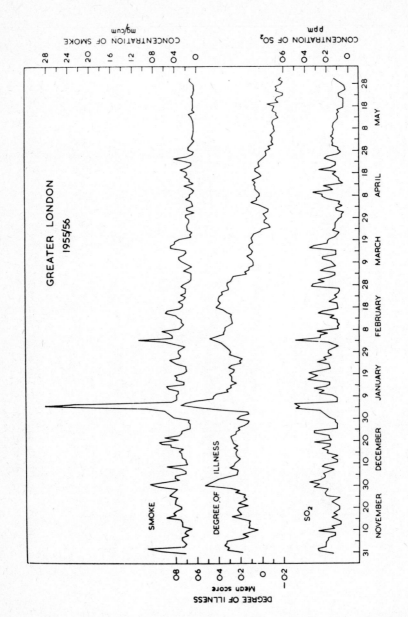

*Fig* 3    Degree of illness and pollution, London 1955-6

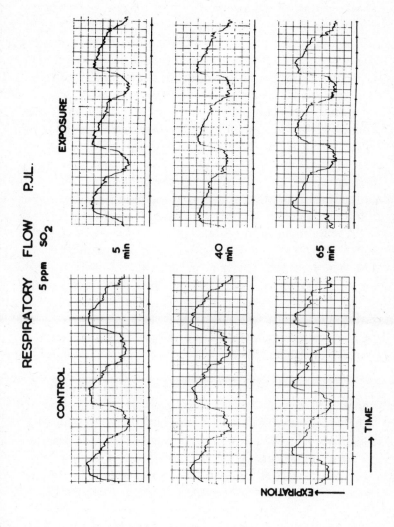

*Fig 4* Variations in flow with time, before and after exposure to 5 ppm. sulphur dioxide

pulmonary artery pressure and heart failure.

In the laboratory, individual pollutants and mixtures of gases and particles, in realistic concentration, are inhaled by healthy volunteers to see if they produce increases in airway resistance or any other disturbances in lung function in an effort to identify the active ingredients of polluted air. Various methods are used; the simplest is the measurement, by means of a lightweight spirometer, of the volume of air blown out in the first second of a forced expiration; a diminution in this quantity after inhalation of an experimental mixture may be related to an increase in the resistance of the airways. A more complicated, but more sensitive, method is by use of the whole body plethysmograph. Another simple technique by which changes in airway resistance may be assessed is by measurement, before and after exposure, of the peak flow rate at the start of a forced expiration. This method has the advantage of simplicity; the instrument is portable, may be used in the home and in surveys. Valuable results have been obtained by patients and colleagues who have made daily measurements throughout the winter and over periods of five years by which some relationship between changes in pollution and lung function have been demonstrated.

These methods have a serious disadvantage in that the mere effort involved in doing the test may produce increases in airway resistance and so obscure the possible effect of a pollutant. Sensitive instruments for measuring flow rates during quiet breathing are available and experiments are in progress in which flow patterns at rest are being analysed before, during, and after the inhalation of test mixtures (Fig 4). The use of the computer in the analysis of these breathing patterns is proving invaluable. We, and other workers in many parts of the world, have carried out thousands of experiments using many different techniques, and have not yet identified in the laboratory the ingredient or mixture of substances responsible for the effects seen clinically when pollution rises. There are, of course, many disadvantages in limiting, for obvious ethical reasons, exposures to normal subjects rather than 'gassing' patients. Perhaps our methods of measurement are too crude and success in the search will come when we have developed new techniques. More fruitful has been our collection, over years, of data on lung functions day by day, from our own and patients'performances, as air pollution has varied 'naturally'. The somewhat selective diminution in pollution where reductions in smoke concentrations have exceeded those of sulphur dioxide has been studied by this method and, as will be shown later, tends to incriminate smoke rather than sulphur dioxide, but it is as yet difficult to take any firm pronouncement, so complex is the problem and so numerous the variables. The search goes on.

Despite the urgency of the need to identify the pollutants responsible for exacerbations of existing disease (so that the emission of these pollutants may be reduced or prohibited), a more important problem is to determine the extent to which pollution is responsible for the development of chronic bronchitis – a disease which, especially in Britain, causes untold suffering and many deaths. In its early simple form, chronic bronchitis is characterised by the hypersecretion of mucus by glands and goblet cells in the wall of the bronchial tubes. In the normal the secretion of mucus needed for keeping the lungs free from contamination and protected from irritation is imperceptible; the patient with chronic bronchitis secretes so much that he needs to cough to clear the the excess – he has a cough productive of clear mucoid phlegm. This phase is related, usually, to irritation and the commonest irritant is inhaled cigarette smoke rather than air polluction. Not without reason simple chronic bronchitis is called 'smoker's cough'. The irritant produces a degree of airway obstruction by a combination of spasm of the bronchial muscles, the deep layer of mucus on the surface of the tubes and the hypertrophic mucosa developed to supply the excess demand for mucus. There are good reasons to believe that if the irritant is removed, if the patient stops smoking, the changes described above may regress and the cough and expectoration cease. All too often, however, simple chronic bronchitis becomes complicated by the establishment of infection. Acute bronchitis with the expectoration of purulent sputum periodically overlies the chronic picture and eventually the infection may become permanently established unless treated with anti biotics. In addition to increasing airways obstruction, destruction of the lung occurs. this being gross in the later stages of emphysema, a disease which is the end result of chronic bronchitis. There would seem to be good reasons for thinking that air pollution is one of the important factors in favouring the development of complicated chronic bronchitis. The results of many epidemiological studies suggest that, apart from worsening the disease, cigarette-smoking is less to blame than air pollution in this later stage, in that in many people it is an evolutionary disease process.

One of the major difficulties which beset those who study the evolution of chronic bronchitis is the fact that the disease may take a long time, even a lifetime, to develop. Another serious difficulty is that, in the development of the disease, in its different stages many factors, including constitutional ones, are involved. Recent work has shown that, in the first year of life, the prevalence of lower respiratory tract infection was closely related to the average pollution in the town of birth, whereas the prevalence of infection of the upper airways, ear, nose and throat, showed no such relationship with pollution.

The temptation to ascribe the development of chronic bronchitis to simple chemical irritation is great, especially when such substances as sulphur dioxide and sulphuric acid, irritating in high concentrations, are found in British urban air. But the facts do not support this simple hypothesis and more subtle mechanisms must be sought.

We have thought that polluted air may favour the establishment of bacteria, either by stimulating the growth of inhaled organisms or by altering the chemical or physical nature of the mucus on which the germs must land. We have found that particulate matter

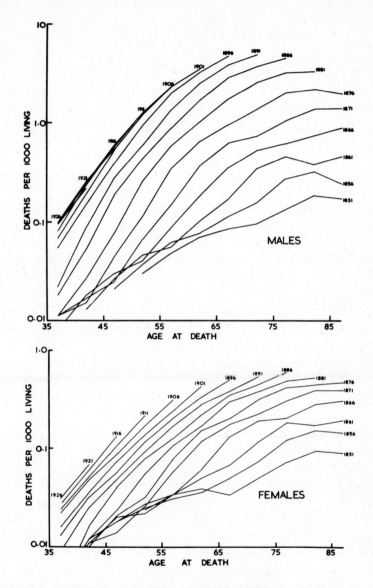

*Fig* 5    Lung cancer mortality, England and Wales.  The lines
show death rates for people born around the years stated

collection from London air inhibits in vitro and would appear to
stimulate the growth of Haemophilus influenzae, an organism
commonly found in the sputum produced by patients with complicated bronchitis. The phenomena we observed, though striking, may
may be of limited relevance to the story of the development of
chronic bronchitis, but it is certain that the mechanisms involved
are no less complex. There is much work to be done on the chemistry of mucus in different individuals and on immunological
aspects of response to pollutants.

Inhalation of urban air has often been blamed for the development of lung cancer. There are attractive reasons for suspecting
that air pollution causes lung cancer. The disease is more prevalent
in towns than in the country; town air contains polycyclic hydrocarbons, some of which are carcinogenic at least to skin and are
derived largely from coal smoke. There are, however, many serious
objections to the simple hypothesis that all the lung cancer in our
midst has been caused by polluted air. We have to ask ourselves the
cause of the alarming rise in the prevalence of lung cancer, not
merely what causes the disease. We must note the fact that the
number of lung cancer deaths in the last decade was only just
exceeded by the number recorded in the first sixty years of this
century. The way in which the disease has increased is clearly dis-
played by cohort analysis, in which death rates among groups of
people born at five-yearly intervals are plotted. It can be seen from
Fig 5 that, in successive cohorts, lung cancer has become progressively a more common disease affecting younger people. These
changes have been seen first among men and later among women.
The rate of increase among men is slowing down, but this
favourable trend is not yet seen among women. The difference
between death rates in town and country, and between mortality
among men and women, is seen in countries, such as Finland and
Norway, where pollution by polycyclic hydrocarbons is very low.
All the evidence points to the emergence of a new factor at about the
turn of the century which acted on an increasing proportion of the

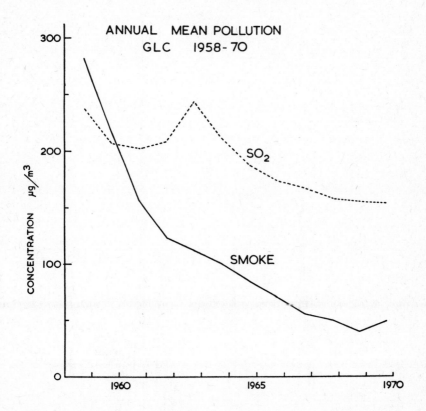

*Fig* 6   Annual mean concentration of smoke and sulphur dioxide, Greater London Council sites, 1958-70

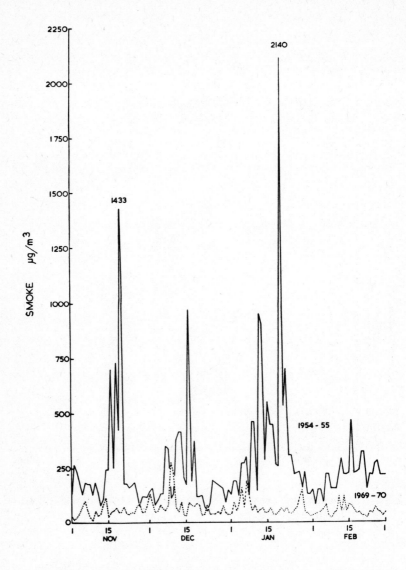

*Fig* 7    Daily smoke concentrations, St Bartholomew's Hospital, winter 1954-5 and 1969-70

population, first on males and later on females. Motor-vehicle exhausts, petrol and diesel, have been held responsible; but were the petrol engine the cause of the observed rise in lung cancer it would have to have produced it with little or no latent period, and one would expect there to be a great excess of lung cancer among those who, by virtue of their occupations, were exposed to much exhaust. Fortunately, we do not find such evidence. The diesel engine was, for some time, a popular scapegoat, but the rise in lung cancer started long before the widespread use of diesel vehicles.

There can be no doubt at all that cigarette smoking, and, to a lesser extent, other forms of tobacco smoking, is the major cause of lung cancer, and there is therefore the strongest case for persuading smokers to abandon the habit and children to avoid acquiring it.

Having indicted cigarette smoke as the overwhelmingly important cause of most lung cancer, one must continue to study other factors which include urban air pollution, either *per se* or in combination with smoking and occupational causes of which several are already recognised.

While we must deplore the misery and waste of life caused by smoking, we have cause to rejoice that in this country air pollution by 'conventional' pollutants is declining dramatically. The Clean Air Act of 1956 wisely tackled smoke, which is always a product of inefficient combustion, rather than wait for evidence of the harm that other pollutants, less readily abateable, could do. The implementation of the Act and its successor, and the voluntary use of more efficient forms of domestic heating, have led to a spectacular reduction of pollution by smoke and to a lesser degree by sulphur dioxide (Fig 6). Some better idea of the degree of progress made in smoke abatement may be obtained from Fig 7, in which we have drawn, on the same chart, concentrations of smoke which we measured at St Bartholomew's Hospital during the winters of 1954-5 and 1969-70.

An unexpected bonus has been the reduction in the number of

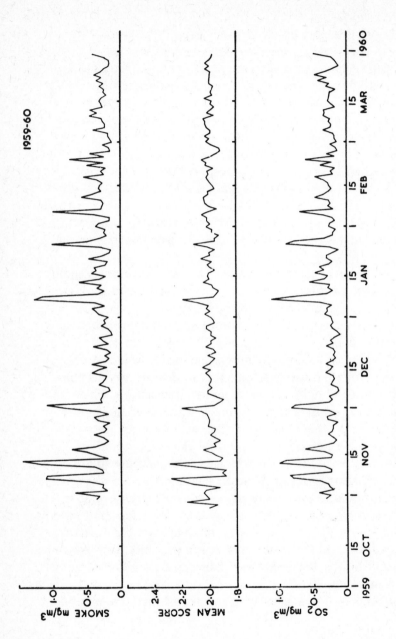

*Fig* 8    Daily changes in the condition of bronchitic patients, London, 1959-60

days in the year when sulphur dioxide concentrations reached $500\mu g/m^3$. We think that this decrease may be due to the fact that in the absence of a pall of morning smoke the sun can warm the earth more rapidly, and break up temperature inversions which might otherwise persist and constitute the old-type 'smog' (Fig 8).

As these improvements have been occurring, we have been persisting with some simple research, the results of which have enabled us to make some assessment of a likely improvement in health. The diary experiments referred to earlier have been repeated at intervals. In the old smoky days we could easily demonstrate a close association between exacerbations of illness and pollution. As time passed and smoke became rarer, the association lessened until during the winter of 1969-70 we saw little more than 'background noise' in the degree of illness of the groups of patients who helped us by filling in their diaries (Figs 9 and 10).

Extreme caution is needed in assessing this type of result; so many factors other than exposure to air pollution are involved in the worsening of respiratory illness. Weather and infection are major influences, but one must also consider improvements in therapeutic measures and the effect of advice not to venture out to work or out of doors when pollution is high. Yet, despite these considerations, there are other pieces of evidence which support the belief that the public health is improving as a result of reductions in pollution. Some of the measurements of respiratory function made daily on ourselves have shown over the years, an improvement rather than the deterioration expected with age. Another encouraging feature, which is subject to reservations similar to those which must restrain us when looking at other evidence, is the decrease in death rates from bronchitis in three cohorts of males; the London rates; from being twice the rural rates in men born in 1905, have fallen in two successive cohorts to a figure only a little greater than that among country dwellers.

As the classic pollutants recede, we must maintain constant vigilance in the face of new emissions from the myriads of

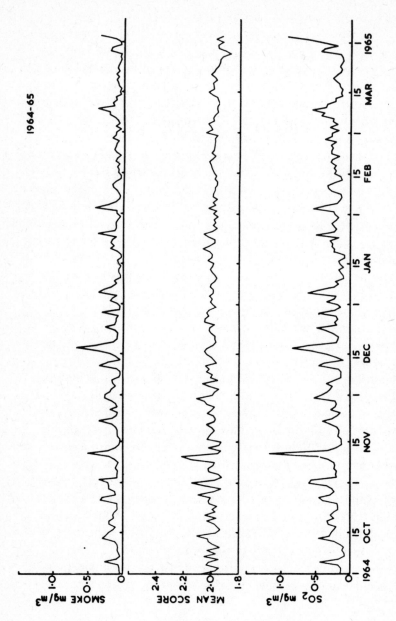

*Fig* 9    Daily changes in the condition of bronchitic patients, London, 1964-5

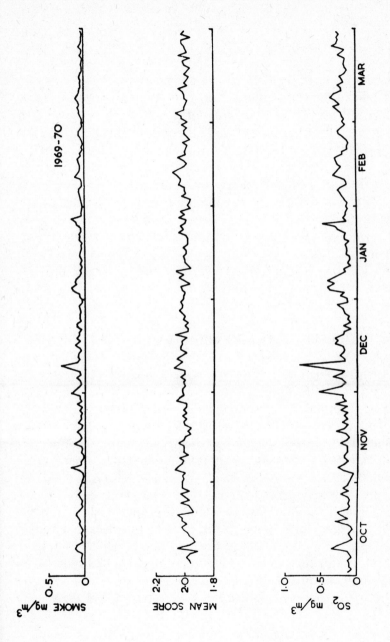

*Fig* 10   Daily changes in the condition of bronchitic patients, London, 1969-70

industrial processes and from motor vehicles. Some general theory
of theory of toxicity or carcinogenicity might enable us to regard
with especial suspicion certain compounds and prohibit, with
appropriate strictness, their discharge into the air. But it is just as
important to remember that in our study of air pollution and our
fight against it we must be careful not to give it a priority which it
cannot merit in existing social and economic circumstances. It is
undoubtedly evil in certain concentrations yet, implicity, is tolerable in come cases, as we tolerate ambient levels of carbon dioxide
and regard it as the highly desirable end product of combustion of
fuels. The cost of abolition of pollution becomes very great as the
concentrations aimed at become lower. To insist on vast expenditure at the expense of other meritorious reforms may yet do harm
to the public health. There are other social evils which must be
fought, and the struggle against pollution must be seen in this
context.


## SOME PROBLEMS IN THE MEASUREMENT OF ATMOSPHERIC POLLUTION *T. D. Davies*

The scientific measurement of atmospheric pollution is an essential
pre-requisite for the development of environmental standards.
Accurate information is required for dosage-response studies, not-
withstanding the especial difficulties inherent in such investigations.
Reliable monitoring of ambient air quality facilitates the implementation of adopted standards. Even if pollutant-emission rates and
characteristics are determinable, it is not possible to rely on diffusion equations and dispersion models for an accurate estimate of
atmospheric concentrations. The simplification of real conditions
to allow mathematical characterisation often proceeds to a degree
where the assumptions render the computations meaningless. In
addition, testing the diffusion models presupposes that reliable
and accurate air-quality data are available.

With present measurement techniques, sampling and analytical errors are rarely less than ten to twenty per cent, and often appreciably greater. The large number of methods in use makes it difficult to compare or interpret environmental quality data collected from different sources. Standardisation of measurement methods is essential. Assuming standardisation, measurement errors are still appreciable and these may be considered most conveniently under three headings:

## Network design errors
Sampling network density must be a function of two considerations: the variability of the pollutant to be examined and the purpose to be served by the network. A study in Nashville determined that at least four stations per square mile would be required to estimate the mean daily concentrations of sulphur dioxide with a ninety-five per cent assurance of ±20 per cent accuracy[1]. The network density should vary with time-scale, surface roughness and pollutant. Most atmospheric pollution surveys utilise a very sparse network even when examining highly variable pollutants over short time periods. The usual procedure of computing isopleths from sampling network data assumes a Laplacian behaviour, whereas the turbulent nature of an urban atmosphere should preclude such assumptions. In some cities quasi-closed atmospheric systems can be physically or thermally induced.

## Sampling technique errors
The site of each sampler must be chosen so that it is representative of the surrounding area. Conditions of this nature are often impossible to fulfil; buildings can disturb the airflow sufficiently to create marked variability in pollutant concentrations over short distances. Under certain conditions sulphur dioxide concentrations on opposite sides of a building are different by an order of magnitude.[2] Similarly, the sulphur dioxide concentration at the top of a high-rise block may be a factor of ten greater than the ground-level concentration. Three-dimensional urban landscapes may

render ground-level concentrations meaningless for a proportion of the population, and it has been suggested that trace substance concentrations in rainfall could give a better estimate of atmospheric pollution.[3] However, unless techniques are devised for neglecting the contributions of exotic pollutants to the trace substance concentrations then errors of several hundred per cent may be incurred.[4] Locational considerations, such as proximity to roads and factories, are of obvious importance. Sites near roads can exhibit smoke concentrations ten times greater than those at a site one hundred metres away;[5] lead concentrations may be six times greater. A sulphur dioxide with the inlet funnel 15cm above a hedge has suffered a daily loss of up to 80 per cent of the gas because of the uptake by the foliage.[6] The author has observed pollution-monitoring equipment with the inlets actually submerged in lilac tree foliage.

The duration of sampling is critical with highly variable pollutants. Hourly mean sulphur dioxide concentrations of 100-200$\mu$g m$^{-3}$ can mask short term pulses of 3-4,000$\mu$gm$^{-3}$.[7] The shortest sampling period reveals the most valuable information but greatly increases data-handling difficulties. Instrument sampling errors may lead to serious discrepancies between observed and real pollutant concentrations. Isokinetic airflow is the only condition under which an aspirated sampler will measure true dosage. This condition is rarely fulfilled, even the presence of the sampling head itself will disturb airflow. An illustration of the effect of non-isokinetic flow is where a difference of a factor of three has been found in pollen collection with an aspirator in upwind and downwind directions in a wind funnel.[8] Another experiment established that the aerosol concentrations collected on a flat-plate sampler at 0.9m height was one third of that collected at ground level.[9] The effect was due to the internal boundary layer developed over the plate and the subsequent disturbance of the airflow and the efficiency of the catch.

Other large sources of error include brass fittings, rubber or deteriorating PVC (all common components of monitoring equipment) which can affect some pollutants. In the standard daily sulphur dioxide instruments, even the use of freshly prepared demineralized water can reduce concentrations by eighty per cent because of the release of carbon dioxide.[10]

Many sampling techniques employ collection in series. It is important that the first collector units do not interfere with subsequent collection. Some of the materials collected on a filter in the first unit may react with some of the gaseous components (eg particulate and gaseous fluoride). There is little doubt that sulphur dioxide is absorbed by a filter and collected material, particularly under moist conditions. Often no account is taken of the sulphuric acid phase in the atmosphere (because of non-collection and interception on filters), which may comprise twenty to thirty per cent of the total sulphur concentrations, and which is possibly critical for effects on human health.

## Chemical analysis errors

Few of the large number of chemical analysis methods available for pollutant determination may be regarded as specific. For example, most of the inorganic gaseous pollutant techniques depend upon approaches (acid base reactions, oxidation-reduction, colorimetric procedures or electrical conductivity) which are non-specific and provide a measure of all absorbed pollutants having similar properties. More specific methods are available, but they are elaborate and difficult to implement. A pertinent example of the non-specificity of an analysis is the hydrogen peroxide method of collecting sulphur dioxide. The presence of other strong acids and alkalis can affect the result. Recent work has indicated that the reduction in the real concentration of sulphur dioxide by amonia may often be greater than the $25\text{-}30\mu\mathrm{gm}^{-3}$ loss stipulated by B.S. 1747.[10] The effect over short-time periods may be considerable.

Difficulties are apparent when the pollutants present in the atmosphere are not the same as those discharged, the pollutants sampled are not the same species as in the atmosphere, and the materials analysed are not the same as the ones collected. The collection and analysis of various pollutants will not provide a picture of the changes occurring in the atmosphere. This problem is manifested in the development of the secondary pollutants of photochemical reactions.

*Conclusion*

Neglect of any of the above considerations may result in measurement errors of several hundred per cent. No criticism of contemporary methods of collection and analysis is intended. With present finance and resources, pollutant measurement techniques are often designed to optimum standards. However, great care must be exercised in formulating environmental standards on the basis of determined atmospheric pollutant concentrations. The unavoidably arbitrary nature of air quality standards is not improved by the use of measurement techniques which enable estimates of pollutants concentration to be made to an order of magnitude only.

## THE BEHAVIOUR OF $SO_2$ AND OTHER GASES IN CROSSING AN AIR-WATER INTERFACE *P. S. Liss*

The rate of transfer of a gas across an air-water interface is inversely proportional to the total resistance to transfer of the gas exhibited by the interface. The total resistance may be interpreted as the sum of the individual resistances of the air and water phases.[11] If for any particular gas, the magnitudes of the two resistances are known, it is possible to ascertain which phase will control the rate of exchange. Unfortunately, most field and laboratory studies yield only values for the total resistance.

One way of overcoming this problem is to simultaneously measure the rate of exchange of water molecules and the dissolved gas being studied. The exchange of water vapour, in common with evaporation-condensation of any pure liquid, is usually assumed to be subject to gas phase resistance alone. This assumption is likely to remain true for most natural waters, provided they do not contain large amounts of surface active material. Thus, from the rate of water vapour exchange, values of the gas phase resistance may be found. By assuming that this is also the value of the gas phase resistance for the gas of interest, the total measured resistance may be split into its two component parts.

Results show that the exchange of gases of low or moderate solubility (eg $O_2$, $CO_2$) is controlled by resistance in the liquid phase.[12] This leads to the relatively long residence time of about seven years for $CO_2$ in the atmosphere.[13] The seven-year residence time for $CO_2$ means that any additional $CO_2$ entering the atmosphere from the burning of fossil fuels will generally be well mixed before crossing the air-sea interface. This explains why, although much of the $CO_2$ from fossil fuel combustion enters the oceans (and the biosphere), measurable increase in the atmosphere level is observed.[14]

In the case of $SO_2$, the liquid phase resistance is decreased relative to that for $O_2$ or $CO_2$, not only because of its considerably greater solubility but also because of the chemical reactivity of the $SO_2$ in water under certain conditions. This decrease in the liquid phase resistance for $SO_2$ means that gas and liquid phase resistances may be of similar magnitude and so both must be considered. The extent of exchange enhancement due to the chemical reactivity of $SO_2$ is dependent on pH. The following table is a simplified version of the one given by Liss[15] and gives values for the gas and liquid phase resistance for $SO_2$ and the ratio of these two resistances, at different pH values. It is based on data for exchange of $SO_2$ at the air-sea interface.

At pH 2.8 both resistances are approximately equal. Below this pH, liquid rather than gas phase resistance controls the exchange. As the pH increases above 2.8 the gas phase resistance becomes increasingly dominant. As noted by Liss,[15] these results are not greatly affected by change in the degree of mixing in the system. Furthermore, they should be applicable to other air-water interfaces in the environment (eg airborne water droplets, lakes, rivers etc), as well as to the air-sea interface. Experimental verification of the change from gas to liquid phase control of $SO_2$ transfer at a

| pH | Gas phase resistance $h \ cm^{-1} \ x \ 10^3$ | Liquid phase resistance $h \ cm^{-1} \ x \ 10^5$ | Gas phase resistance / liquid phase resistance |
|----|----|----|----|
| 2   | 8.8 | 3700 | 0.24   |
| 2.8 | 8.8 | 855  | 1.03   |
| 3   | 8.8 | 560  | 1.57   |
| 4   | 8.8 | 59   | 14.92  |
| 5   | 8.8 | 7.3  | 120.6  |
| 6   | 8.8 | 3.5  | 251.4  |
| 7   | 8.8 | 3.4  | 258.8  |
| 8   | 8.8 | 3.4  | 258.8  |
| 9   | 8.8 | 3.4  | 258.8  |

pH between 2 and 3 is given in the recent paper by Brimblecombe and Spedding,[16] and from work in progress in this University.

The pHs of most natural waters at the surface of the earth fall in the range 4 to 9. Thus for virtually all environmental air-water interfaces the exchange of $SO_2$ should be subject to control by gas phase resistance. From this it can be argued that the behaviour of $SO_2$ in exchanging between the atmosphere and natural waters should resemble that of water vapour rather than $CO_2$ or $O_2$. Three tentative conclusions may be drawn from this result:

  i Vertical gradients of $SO_2$ and water vapour close to the sea surface should be of similar magnitude.
  ii $SO_2$ gas should be taken up rapidly by airborne water droplets. This has important implications in the monitoring of atmospheric $SO_2$ levels if the samplers used incorporate filters which may trap water droplets.
  iii The mean residence time of an $SO_2$ molecule in the

atmosphere should be about the same as that for a water molecule (ten days[17]). This contrasts with the much longer residence time for a $CO_2$ molecule (seven years), where exchange is controlled by resistance in the liquid phase. A residence time of about ten days for $SO_2$ is in reasonable agreement with the value of five days given by Junge.[17] In using the residence time concept for $SO_2$, two other factors should be borne in mind. Firstly, because $SO_2$ is known to adsorb very rapidly on solid surfaces, air-solid as well as air-water exchange should be considered. Secondly, because the atmosphere is not well mixed with respect to $SO_2$ the residence time concept is not strictly applicable.

*Topics for further study include:*
1    Measurements of *in situ* exchange rates for both the air-sea interface and other natural air-water interfaces.
2    Studies, in different environments, of the relative roles of transfer across gas-liquid and gas-solid interfaces, in the removal of gases such as $SO_2$ from the atmosphere.
3    Determination of the fate and effect of $SO_2$ and other gases after absorption by natural waters of various types.


## THE POSSIBLE ROLE OF NATURAL SUSPENDED MATTER IN CONTROLLING THE LEVELS OF DISSOLVED CONSTITUENTS IN ESTUARIES AND COASTAL WATERS  *P. S. Liss*

In most United Kingdom estuaries there is fairly rapid mixing between river and sea water. If the only process occurring is straightforward physical mixing of the fresh and saline water, the concentration of any particular dissolved constituent in the estuarine water should bear a simple linear relationship to a conservative index of mixing, such as salinity. However, if during mixing in the estuary chemical or biological processes are operative, then the relationship between the concentration of dissolved species and

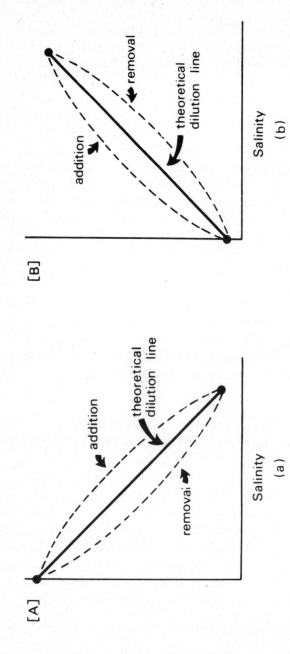

*Fig* 11    Idealised graphs of the variation with salinity of dissolved components in estuarine waters: (a) dissolved component richer in river water than sea water (b) dissolved component richer in sea water than river water

salinity may deviate from linearity. Figures 11 (a) and (b) are idealised representations of the various possibilities.

If removal of the measured component occurs, the observations should fall below the straight line joining the points corresponding to 100 per cent river water and 100 per cent sea water (theoretical dilution line). Conversely, if addition takes place the points should lie above the theoretical dilution line. Fig 11 (a) is for a dissolved component which occures in higher concentration in river water than in sea water. Fig 11 (b) illustrates the more usual case in which the sea water concentration of the species studied is greater than that in river water.

The relationship between salinity and concentration has been examined for very few components. Of these the best studied is dissolved silicon, which generally occurs in greater concentration in river water than in sea water. A linear relationship has been found in a number of estuaries, and this has been interpreted as indicating straightforward mixing of the fresh and saline water. However, Bien *et al*, working on the Mississippi, observed substantial removal of dissolved silicon during mixing in this estuary.[18] Liss and Spencer found removal of 10-20 per cent for dissolved silicon in the Conway estuary in North Wales.[19] Results from one of these surveys of the Conway are shown in Fig 12.

From their laboratory and field studies, Liss and Spencer were able to confirm the conclusion of Bien *et al* that the removal was due to sorption of dissolved silicon on to suspended sediment in the estuary. Almost complete removal of dissolved silicon has been reported by Wollast and de Broeu for the Scheldt estuary in Belgium.[20] However, a large part of this removal is probably due to large-scale utilisation of dissolved silicon by phytoplankton, in this heavily polluted estuary.

Recent work on the estuary of the River Alde in Suffolk, carried out from these laboratories,[21] has shown that removal may also occur for dissolved boron. This element is generally more concentrated in sea water than in river water. These results are shown in

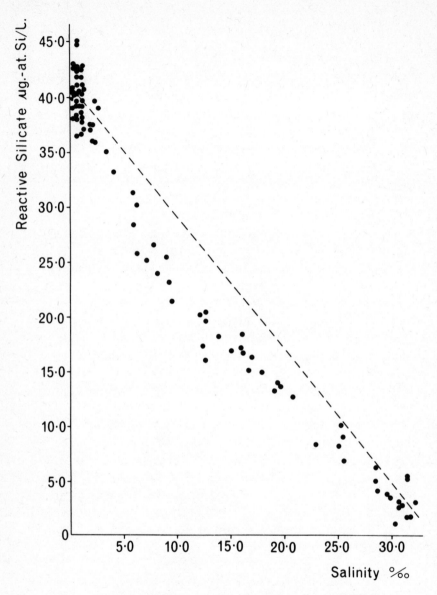

*Fig* 12    Variation of dissolved silicon concentration with salinity
in the Conway estuary, North Wales. The theoretical
dilution line is shown dotted. (From Liss & Spencer[19])

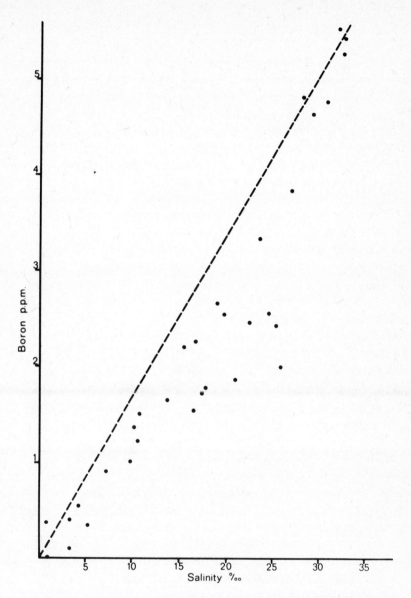

*Fig* 13    Variation of dissolved boron concentration with salinity
in the estuary of the River Alde, Suffolk. The theoretical
dilution line is shown dotted. (From Liss & Pointon[21])

Fig 13.

Most of the points corresponding to samples of intermediate
salinity lie below the theoretical dilution line. In this case, the
boron is presumably being removed from the sea water rich in
boron coming into the estuary.

The relationship between dissolved phosphorous and salinity
has been studied in a number of estuaries. In some cases there is
a reasonably good inverse relationship with salinity. However, in
other estuaries there appears to be a tendency, at least over part of
the salinity range, for the dissolved phosphorous concentrations
to be invariant with salinity ie, for samples of different salinity to
have very similar dissolved phosphorous concentrations. It has
been suggested that in such estuaries there is some 'buffer' mechanism operating to control the dissolved phosphorous levels.

Strong evidence for this suggestion comes from the work on the
Tamar estuary in Devon carried out by Butler and Tibbitts.[22]
Some of their results are shown in Fig 14.

Samples were collected on two surveys in the seaward end of
the Tamar estuary (Stations 1-10), and analysed for total dissolved
nitrogen and phosphorus as well as salinity. The two surveys were
separated by a fortnight, during which time there was exceptionally
heavy rainfall. This can be seen from the fact that at most stations
the salinity has decreased by up to one-third between the two
surveys. The total dissolved nitrate shows a good inverse relationship with the salinity. This is due to the large amount of fresh
water added to the estuary being very rich in dissolved nitrate
derived from land drainage. Although the drainage water is also
likely to contain large amounts of dissolved phosphorus, no change
was observed in the levels of dissolved phosphorus between the
two surveys. Butler and Tibbitts interpret this observation in terms
of reactions, involving suspended sediment and dissolved phosphorus,
'buffering' the phosphate levels in the estuary. They also report
laboratory tests which indicate that estuarine sediment is able to
bring about such buffering.

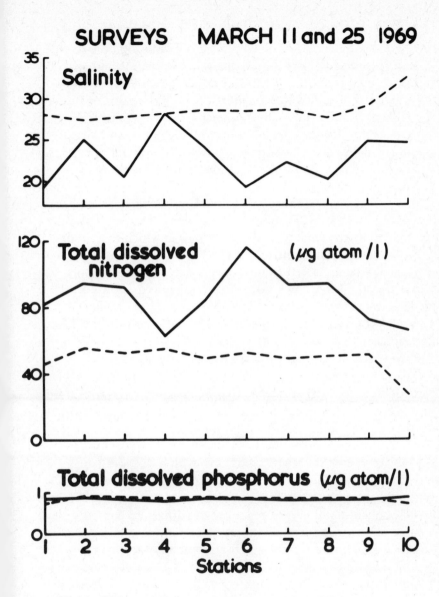

*Fig* 14　Variation of salinity, total dissolved nitrogen and total dissolved phosphorus found on two surveys of the Tamar estuary, Devon. (From Butler & Tibbits[22])

If reactions between dissolved phosphorus and solid phases are important in controlling phosphate levels in estuarine and coastal waters, this has important implications for the disposal of phosphate and nitrate rich wastes in such waters. The results of Butler and Tibbitts indicate that a buffer mechanism may exist for phosphate, but not for nitrate. Thus levels of nitrate in saline waters will increase in direct proportion to the amount injected, whereas phosphate levels may tend to show a lesser or zero increase.

In this context, present moves in the United States to replace detergents containing phosphorus compounds as builders (usually sodium tripolyphosphate), by formulations in which the builder is a compound containing nitrogen (eg NTA - nitrilotriacetate), seem misguided. When released to the aqueous environment, tripolyphosphates and NTA break down to give dissolved phosphorus and nitrogen respectively, in forms which are readily assimilated by phytoplankton. Apart from the possible health hazards of NTA, there appears to be no buffer mechanism in the aquatic environment to lessen the impact on plankton growth of the nitrogen compounds produced from its degradation. Furthermore, Ryther and Dunston have recently suggested that in some coastal waters it is the availability of nitrogen rather than phosphorus which limits the phytoplankton bloom.[23]

Although most work so far has concentrated on plant nutrient elements (N,P and Si), reactions involving estuarine sediments may well be important for many other elements (eg trace metals) in solution. Further research is required in order to elucidate the possible role of natural solid phases in estuarine and coastal waters in controlling the levels of dissolved species in such waters. These solids may constitute a major sink for potentially harmful substances introduced into the aqueous environment. If this is the case, then it is important to know the capacity of this reservoir for particular elements, and whether there are any circumstances in which the material associated with the sediments may be released back into the water.

Notes to this chapter are on page 195

# 3: The Economic and Social Inputs

In this chapter Professor Beckerman develops the thesis that there is an economic optimum in the control of pollution. It does not pay a community to produce goods the value of which is less than the combined cost of resources used in their production and of the pollution that accompanies it; or to abate pollution to a point at which the cost of abatement exceeds the benefit. He suggests that these considerations can, with advantage, be translated into practice by fiscal means of regulation, ie by taxing pollution or subsidising its abatement. He ends with some remarks about the probable effect on the economy of the United Kingdom of the optimum abatement of pollution. Professor Hill elaborates the principle of an optimum abatement of pollution, and examines the effects of pollution control on economic growth. Dr MacDonald describes the approach of the United States government to the use of fiscal methods of controlling pollution, and gives some figures illustrating the likely effect of pollution control on the United States economy. Mr Langley examines the probable consequences to industry of requiring external costs to be embodied in the price of the product, and discusses the problem set by technological advances taking place in advance of full scientific knowledge of the consequences for the environment of their being exploited. Dr Young examines the use of cost-benefit analysis for reaching decisions when the course under consideration would produce irreversible consequences

These papers produced considerable discussion, which is summarised at the end of the chapter, about the scope for using fiscal measures of control, the application of cost-benefit analysis and the competition for resources between protection of the environment and other social objectives.


## POLLUTION CONTROL: WHO SHOULD PAY? HOW? HOW MUCH? *W. Beckerman*

*Why there is a problem*
First it is necessary to put pollution into perspective. Pollution imposes costs to society — either in order to remove it, or to put up with it, and hence with reduced standards of living. But nearly all output is produced at a cost, including the labour costs of the disutility (to most people) of work. We do not, on that account, urge that all output should cease in order that the costs be eliminated. The social optimum output merely requires that the costs involved in the production of any commodity (at the margin) do not exceed the benefits (at the margin) which society obtains from that production.

But pollution costs tend to fall on the victims, not on the polluter. For example, the costs of laundry to remove smoke from factory chimneys is met by the victims one way or another, and do not enter into the costs of production of the owner of the chimney. Hence (a) the output of products, the production of, or consumption of, which generates pollution tends to be pushed too far, and (b) the use of polluting techniques of production is not discouraged either.

If the producer has a free and unrestricted right to pollute, this facility can be regarded as a free input into the production process. In other words, he is producing with the aid of an input — disposal facilities for his smoke — that costs him nothing. Obviously, in

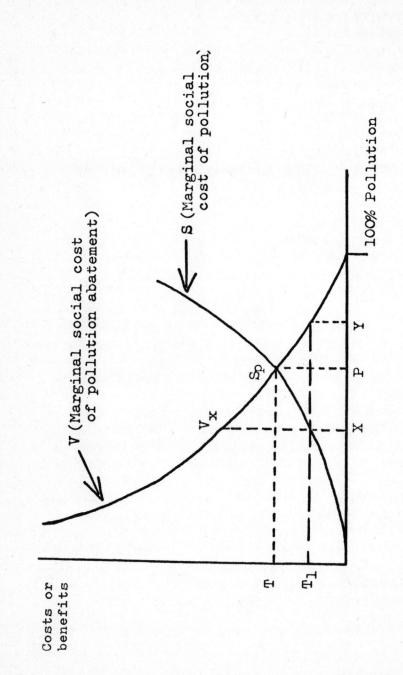

such a situation he will tend to be extravagant with this input and
not seek a technique of production which economises in his use of
this facility.

The problem of pollution is not how to stop it altogether, but
how to reduce it to the 'optimum' point. This is where the social
costs of further abatement would exceed the social costs (at the
margin) of the remaining pollution. This is the optimum level of
pollution — and it is quite distinct from the question of who should
bear the social costs of pollution at the optimum. The latter issue
is a matter of income distribution and equity, and is nothing to do
with the question of what is optimum output. (This is a simplification, of course, since the income distribution affects the relative
prices and costs in society that are used as a reference point for
deciding what is optimum output).

Thus there are two problems in connection with the optimum
control of pollution. First, there is the problem of defining and
measuring the relevant costs and benefits. Secondly, there is the
problem of the best means of attaining optimum pollution — eg
by taxes or by direct regulation.

As regards the former, if failing to abate pollution leads to no
expense or other penalty to the polluters, they will not abate at all
(leaving aside social conscience, etc). In terms of the above diagram,
therefore, pollution will be 100 per cent, with possibly high social
costs of the pollution as measured by the 'S' curve at the point
where it cuts the right hand vertical axis. (Hundred per cent
pollution here merely means that there is no abatement so that
pollution is 100 per cent of what producers find it profitable to
incur in the course of production of the goods. In terms of the
particular polluted environment — a river, or an ocean or an atmospheric area — the pollution may be well below harmful level).
Optimum pollution is at point 'P' where the two curves intersect.
Clearly, if pollution were to be reduced even further to, say, 'X',
the (marginal) social cost of the abatement, as measured by '$XV_x$'
is much higher than the (marginal) cost to society of that level of

pollution, as measured by the height of the 'S' curve at the same
level of pollution. In other words, society has pushed pollution
abatement to the point where the abatement 'PX' has costs that
exceed the social costs of 'PX' pollution.

There are, however, numerous difficulties about this over-simp-
lified discussion of the optimum, including the following:

1    There are many ways of evaluating the 'V' curve. For
example, it is not necessarily equal to the costs that *the
private producer* would have to incur to abate pollution.
Account must also be taken of the scope for some collective
form of abatement or remedial action to be taken. A reduced
supply of the 'bad' polluted water is economically equivalent
to an increase in the supply of the 'good' purified water. The
supply curves of both have to be added together to arrive at
the total social supply curve of pollution abatement. For
purposes of simplification, however, the scope for collective
action can be ignored in the following discussion (without
prejudice to any of the substantive conclusions).

2    There is the tricky question of income distribution and
the fact that (a) different income distributions will imply
different relative prices and costs, and hence change the
optimum and (b) moves to the optimum from a sub-optimum
will itself change the income distribution.

3    There are exceptionally difficult problems of measuring
the costs to society of the pollution (ie the 'S' curve). For
example, recreational effects and health effects are very
difficult to measure, and even to conceptualise clearly.

4    The 'S' curve also raises very tricky problems of how to
deal with the preferences of future generations (a special
aspect of the income distribution issue) or with the risk and
uncertainty problem, particularly in a situation in which
scientific knowledge of environmental consequence is so
shaky.

*Pollution charges, subsidies or 'bribes'*

But, assuming one has decided what level of pollution one wants to achieve (say 'OP'), the problem is to know what is the best way of getting there. To most economists, even those of us who are deeply suspicious of the frequently exaggerated virtues of the price mechanism, it still seems best, in principle, to use the price mechanism to check pollution. If polluters have to pay the cost to society of their pollution then the facility to pollute is no longer free to them and they will, insofar as they seek to maximise profits, have an incentive to carry out only the socially optimum amount of pollution, neither more nor less.

Consider, for example, the case where, in the light of some knowledge or guesses as to the shape of the 'S' and 'V' curves in the above diagram, the optimum level of pollution is thought to be 'OP', where the costs to society of that pollution equals $PS_p$ (=OT). Suppose a tax equal to OT per unit of pollution is imposed on producers. Then producers would have an incentive to reduce pollution to the optimum amount. For if they stopped at, say point 'Y', the marginal tax they still pay is greater than the cost to them of a further reduction in pollution (the tax is higher than the 'V' curve at the pollution level 'Y'). Hence they would be better off if they reduced pollution further, since what they incur in costs of doing so is less than what they gain in not paying so much tax. For every unit by which they reduce pollution, up to the point 'P', they reduce their tax payment by more than they add to their other costs, and hence they save money. But they would not have any incentive to reduce pollution below the optimum point, since below this point the 'V' curve is higher than the tax, so that it would cost them more to further reduce pollution than they would gain from reduced tax payments. In short, a tax equal to what the social costs of pollution would be at the optimum level of pollution tends to engender the optimum level of pollution.

It should be noted that the same result is produced with other variants of the price mechanism, including, strangely enough, a subsidy (some would call it a 'bribe') to polluters based on the extent to which they reduce pollution. For example, suppose, in the above case, the optimum tax, equal to 'OT' is £5 per ton of pollutant. But suppose the government agreed to pay producers £5 for every ton by which they reduced pollution. The result would be the same, for producers would have an incentive to cut pollution until the costs to them of doing so were greater than £5 per ton. Up to that point they gain more from the subsidy than it costs them to reduce pollution, in the same way that, up to that point, they gained more from tax reductions than it cost them to reduce pollution.

This result is clearer if one looks at the polluter as somebody who wastes 'clean air' in his production process, but if he is paid £5 per ton of pollution abatement he can now, in effect, 'sell clean air' at £5 per ton. He will do so up to the point where his costs of producing clean air (ie his cost of pollution abatement) are greater than the £5 per ton price he receives for this new product. To pay him £5 for every unit of clean air that he produces will achieve the same result as taxing him £5 for every unit of clean air that he wastes (ie every unit of dirty air that he produces). And the same result is achieved whoever pays the polluters to reduce pollution – irrespective of whether it is a government subsidy or whether the victims have to compensate the polluters! In each case, optimum pollution will result, but the three methods have very different implications for income distribution or equity.

For example, one of the possible undesirable effects of the subsidy method is that it creates an incentive for people to set up in business solely in order to be potential polluters and thereby qualify for the bribe not to pollute. A quite unnecessary demand for 'clean air' is created. Pollution, or the threat of it, becomes a sort of blackmail. But, of course, there may be exceptions and the final decision is nothing to do with economic optimisation but with value judgments. For example, what about the case where some polluting factory was on the spot first and then a lot of people come along and build houses! On the other hand, one might

take the view that it all depends on whether it is the polluters or
the victims who are poorest and so who can least afford the costs
of abatement.

## Charges versus Direct Regulation

The main advantage of the price mechanism in some form or
other, by comparison with direct regulation of pollution, is that
it tends to minimise the costs of any given degree of pollution
abatement, which is not the same thing as ensuring the optimum
degree of abatement *given those costs.* For (a) it provides an incentive for pollution to be reduced in the most economical manner in
each firm and (b) it leads to the reduction of pollution being concentrated on those firms that can most cheaply reduce it. Both
these effects mean that the social costs of pollution abatement are
minimised, so that the 'V' curve is, effectively, the minimum social
costs of abatement. As regards the former effect, if a pollution
charge (or tax) is imposed each firm can find the most economical
means of minimising the burden of the charge. Some may simply
be forced to reduce output, eg they pass on the tax in higher prices,
so that the demand for their produce is reduced. But for nearly all
firms the pollution content per unit of output is not absolutely
inflexible, so that they can change their techniques of production.
There is evidence recently that, in some cases, the introduction of
pollution charges has led to rapid and/or massive switches in
technique. (During the past few years, in Sweden, mercury
pollution has been almost completely designed out of chlorine and
paper production, and the volume of waste produced from paper
production has also been reduced by a factor of several hundred)
Each firm will try to find the cheapest way of reducing pollution
and hence the economy will gain in that the most economical
means of abatement will be found; whereas if, for example, a
regulation had been laid down to the effect that, in order to reduce
a certain form of air pollution, all firms must increase the height
of their chimneys by so much, or achieve a given reduction in the

sulphur content of their fuel input and so on, in many firms this
will not represent the cheapest way of reducing pollution.

The second effect is similar in character. If all firms are charged
the true social (marginal) cost of pollution of £5 per ton as in the
above example, then some firms may be able to reduce pollution
very cheaply by a substantial amount, so that they will have an
incentive to do so rather than pay the £5 per ton tax. In other
firms, the costs of abatement may rise very steeply and firms may
soon find that after having carried out only a little abatement their
costs of further abatement are higher than £5 per ton. Such firms
will abate very little. Thus, abatement will tend to be concentrated
on firms whose social costs of abatement are low, and only little
abatement will be carried out by firms whose costs of abatement
are high. And this is clearly socially desirable. In all firms there is
an incentive to abate up to the point where the marginal costs of
abatement are equal to the tax and this is obviously the point at
which the total social costs of abatement (at the margin) are lowest.

Contrast this with a direct regulation such as, for example, that
all firms must reduce pollution by 50 per cent. Some firms might
find it very expensive to carry out any large scale abatement so
that by reducing pollution by as much as 50 per cent they would
have to go well beyond the point where their costs of abatement
were above the social costs of the pollution that was thereby
avoided. Society must clearly lose in cases where the social costs
of the abatement are higher than the social costs of the pollution
abated. And other firms may be in the opposite position; namely,
that they could have easily reduced pollution by more than 50 per
cent at a cost less than the social costs of the pollution, but since
they have only been asked to reduce it by 50 per cent why try to
do even better? In such cases society loses in the opposite manner;
namely, the social costs of pollution remain greater than the costs
that would have been incurred by reducing it further. Thus a direct
regulation of this type is clearly suboptimal.

In view of the apparent superiority of the price mechanism as a

means of minimising the social costs of reaching the optimum
amount of pollution, one must ask why there is a preference among
public bodies for the direct regulation? When the possibility of
some sort of tax on pollution is raised the reaction is usually one
of: 'But that would amount to giving a licence to pollute'.

Of course, the 'Licence to pollute' argument in no way refutes
the economic argument, advanced above, for the optimisation
effect of the pollution tax. It would appear, at first sight, that the
objection to a pollution tax must reflect a more basic fallacy;
namely, that *all* pollution is bad, so that insofar as the imposition
of a tax will not lead to the complete elimination of pollution, the
polluter is paying a bribe to be allowed to continue with some
pollution, and that is still too much by comparison with none at
all. But, as far as the British authorities are concerned, it is clear
that they are very conscious of the cost side of pollution abatement. Mr Ireland, the Chief Alkali Inspector, is quite explicit that
the aim of the Alkali Inspectorate in England is 'to clean the air,
not to purify it'.[2] The objection to the tax/charge system may,
instead, be based on the notion that the tax will not reduce at all
or not reduce it to the optimum amount.[3]

There is no evidence for the former, indeed there is plenty of
evidence that any tax on *any* input (which, as explained above, is
what pollution facilities amount to) reduces the use of that input.
And there is now some evidence that a tax on pollution leads to a
considerable cut in pollution.[4]

If it is argued that pollution will be reduced but not by the
optimum amount, then this must be based on one of two possible
assumptions. First, that producers do not respond to taxes, or
other costs, in a manner which more or less maximises their
profits. There is no evidence for this and even if it is true it
would be necessary to establish whether this applies only to a
pollution tax or whether it applies to all taxes and, indeed, to all
costs, in which case there are far more serious problems of resource
misallocation to worry about than the resource misallocation arising

out of externalities!

The second possibility is that it is known that the level of tax that would be imposed in specific cases would not reduce pollution to the known optimum level. For example, it might be thought that a tax of 'OT$_1$' would only reduce pollution to 'OY', (which exceeds the optimum level OP). But that merely means that the tax is not high enough. In general, if it is thought that a given tax will not reduce pollution to the optimum amount this merely means that the tax should be raised.

In fact, direct regulations and controls in this area are probably as economically inefficient as the use, in Soviet economies, of quantitative targets for production to which all firms have to sub-scribe. The result is that some firms produce more than they should produce, given their costs, and others less than they should. Also, the market cannot direct resources into uses where they confer maximum benefits to society since the price mechanism is not allowed to fulfil its usual function of signalling where there is a shortage and where there is a surplus, and of encouraging resources to move from the latter to the former. However, there are signs that attitudes to the use of charges instead of direct regulation are changing. For example, President Nixon's Council on Environmental Quality has recently stated in its annual report that: 'Pollution charges would provide a strong abatement incentive and would tie environmental costs to the processes that generate the pollution'. Several bills to enforce payment according to the amount of pollution are to be presented to Congress during the coming months. There are reports that some of these proposals are now likely to be supported by 'anti-pollution zealots', who tended to regard the proposed tax as a 'licence to pollute', and who now realise that an anti-pollution tax is likely to be far more effective as an incentive to curb pollution than are the controls which they have favoured and which so far have not been very effective.[5]

Of course, there are many difficulties in practice in applying any sort of control scheme based on the quantity of the pollutant or some proxy for it. For example, if producers are subject to charges or regulations related to the amount of their pollution, it must be possible to measure the amount of their pollution. This is often extremely difficult. If, however, they are told what changes to make in their production technique, eg to fit a certain kind of afterburner to their automobiles or to meet certain specifications for chimney heights or flues used, there is less need for frequent supervision. On the other hand, there is the loss arising from the lack of incentive to firms to find the most economical means of reducing pollution. Thus it would be preferable to regulate or tax the pollutant that the after-burners or filter chimneys are designed to reduce.

But in some cases it is socially better to bear this loss since the costs of the alternative control mechanism (whether by means of taxes or quantitative controls) may be greater. In such cases the 'V' curve *including monitoring costs* is raised above what the 'V' curve would be if some other system of control, involving less monitoring costs, were used. Thus it might be better to sub-optimise with a lower 'V' curve than to optimise with a higher 'V' curve.

## The economic 'burden' of pollution abatement

What is the effect on national income and, possibly, on growth, of anti-pollution policies? In brief, if pollution abatement leads to a diversion of resources from final output to intermediate output (ie from satisfying final demand for consumption or investment to providing extra inputs into the productive sector) then national income, in 'real terms' will fall by the amount of the diversion. This should be a once-for-all fall, however, except that:

1    The implementation of the measures would not be immediate so that there might be no absolute fall at all, merely a slower rate of growth until optimum pollution has been attained, after which the growth rate need not be any different from what it was before.

2    Insofar as some of the diversion from final demand was

from investment, rather than consumption, the longer-run
growth rate might also be reduced, but assuming that the
distribution of the cut in final output between consumption
and investment was optimal this does not mean that the
growth of economic 'welfare' in this case is less than in the
case where the whole of the cut is, in the first instance, on
consumption. For in the case where the whole of the cut falls
on investment it must follow that the subsequent slower
growth of consumption was thought to be preferable to the
more immediate greater loss of consumption.

There are two aspects of the 'burden' that should be mentioned
here. First, insofar as the imposition of charges leads to a reduction
in 'real' national income (though it may rise in current prices on
account of a price increase) this does not mean that there is a reduction in economic welfare; on the contrary. Insofar as there is a
move to the optimum pattern of output (not only in terms of the
pattern of final output but also in terms of how much resources
are diverted from final demand to intermediate output) then
economic welfare is increased even if national income falls. This is
because even in 'real' terms, ie after adjusting for changes in the
price level, national income is not a good measure of economic
welfare. There are many reasons for this, one of which being that
some costs will fail to be netted out in the process of arriving at
the estimate (or, indeed, even the concept) of national product,
insofar as they are external costs that fall on the ordinary individual
and not on the 'productive' sector of the economy. GNP does not
include any measure of environmental damage, for example, so that
if GNP is reduced as a result of measures to reduce the amount of
smoke falling on housewives' laundry, the loss of GNP would be
recorded but not the gain in welfare of the housewives (or the
people who suffer less from bronchitis or emphysema, and so on).

Second, there is the question of how big would be the cut in
GNP anyway.

It is difficult to say what the order of magnitude of all this amounts to. But scattered estimates of the costs of pollution abatement programmes in respect of certain countries suggest that the order of magnitude must be about 2 per cent of GNP (equal to one-half of the annual increase in GNP in most countries). Of course, some countries and industries would be affected very much more than others. Also it is impossible to form any clear idea as to how far the sort of estimates available relate to an 'optimum' degree of pollution abatement.

### *The share of pollution abatement costs in national product*

It is impossible to say what proportion of national product any one country should spend on pollution abatement without knowing what is the optimum amount of pollution abatement for all the major forms of pollution in that country. This requires a detailed knowledge of the costs of pollution and of pollution abatement in that country for each major kind of pollution. Obviously such knowledge is not at our disposal for any country. But the following fragments of information might help obtain a reasonably useful rough idea of the orders of magnitude involved - ie are we talking about 1 per cent of national product or 20 per cent of national product? Even allowing for the fact that the figures referred to below (a) related mainly to other countries which may have completely different optimum levels of pollution abatement than the UK, and (b) do not necessarily even reflect optimum pollution levels in the other countries to begin with, it would appear that the order of magnitude is far nearer to 1 per cent of GNP than 20 per cent. In fact a figure of 2 per cent would probably be very much on the 'safe' side.

First, there is an estimate by the person who is probably the world's top authority on pollution economics, Allen Kneese, to the effect that in the USA the cost of 'making substantial improvements on all fronts (air, water, solids — including a lot of cleaning up of problems inherited from the past) would be between $11 billion and $19 billion per annum in 1972-3, when the USA

national product would be about $1,100 billion (at the prices
corresponding to those at which he was making his estimates), so
that the cost of the programme would amount to between 1 per
cent and 1.8 per cent of GNP.[6]

This may appear surprisingly low given the extent to which
pollution has been allowed to get out of hand in many cities, lakes
and rivers in the USA, but, in fact, it appears consistent with some
earlier figures that are actually lower than Kneese's figures which
probably do not embrace such a wide coverage. For example, some
estimates in the *Harvard Business Review*[7] (which draw partly on
official estimates[8] of the cost of reducing air pollution) suggested
that the total expenditures on anti-pollution equipment should
amount to $275 billion by the end of the century. Assuming a 3.5
per cent pa growth rate of GNP in the USA, this means that
pollution control expenditures covered would amount to only 0.45
per cent of GNP. This figure is less than half the Kneese figure, but
it relates only to the costs of anti-pollution equipment and
would not include, for example, the extra current costs of switching
to a low sulphur fuel (which is more expensive than high sulphur
oil).

Also, the *Harvard Business Review* estimates for air pollution
abatement costs seem to be closely in line with one subsequent
official US estimate for this part of total costs given by the US
Secretary of Health, Education and Welfare.[9] This source gives a
figure of about $2.5 billion to be spent on the abatement of air
pollution by government and industry by 1974 which would represent about 0.25 per cent of national product by that year and
which is not much higher than the share for air pollution abatement
implied in the *Harvard Business Review* figures.

In any case, whilst none of these estimates is conceptually the
same as any of the others, they are grouped about an order of
magnitude of 1 per cent of GNP, which is almost the same as the
figure of 1.1 per cent reported in the *US News and World Report*
recently. [10] The air pollution abatement component in these

estimates also matches those given by a senior official of the
*National Center for Air Pollution* in the US Public Health Service,
in which the corresponding expenditures were thought to be of the
order of magnitude of one half of 1 per cent of value added in
manufacturing industry.[11] They are also consistent with the implications of a completely different approach to the problem, namely,
that used by Wassily Leontief in a recent study which estimated,
amongst other things, the effects on prices of ninety individual
industries, of conformity to the 1967 Clean Air Act standards.[12]
Out of these ninety industries, the effect was less than 1 per cent
in 75 cases, between 1 and 5 per cent in 13 cases, between 5 and
10 per cent in 3 cases and above 10 per cent in only one case.
The weighted average for all the 90 industries is below 1 per cent
and insofar as this measures the extra resources used by industry
to meet the air pollution standards laid down in the 1967 Act it is
a measure of the loss of real resources available for other uses.

The only higher figure that I am aware of is probably, however,
a much more authoritative estimate. This is in the second annual
report of the US Council on Environmental Quality, where it is
estimated that the cost of achieving the desired improvement in
the environment of the USA by 1975 will be $105 billion over the
next five years, which is just under 2 per cent of GNP. These
estimates are among the most recent and also appear to be the
most detailed and carefully calculated.

For Japan, a recent estimate[13] is actually accompanied by a
diagram like the one in this paper in order to make the point that
the relevant expenditure for pollution abatement is that at which
the level of abatement is at optimum point. At this level it is
suggested that the total expenditures of a capital nature would be
1.2 per cent of GNP in Japan. But it is not clear what the *annual*
charges would be given the depreciation rate, the required gross
capital formation in anti-pollution equipment in subsequent years,
and the current operating costs. Given that Japan is well known to
have reached an acute situation from the pollution point of view,

the figure would appear to be modest, even allowing for the uncertainties of interpretation just mentioned. Nevertheless a modest
figure of this order of magnitude actually seems on the high side
compared with the published estimate of the expenditure required
over the next ten years, to 'clean up' the Japanese environment.
This is that it will cost £3,500 million over the ten-year period. At
an annual rate this is only £350 million, which is only 0.5 per cent
of Japan's 1970 GNP, and would be only about 0.3 per cent of
1975 GNP.[14]

For the UK such scattered pieces of information that are readily
available suggest that the right figure must also, surprisingly enough,
be of similar order of magnitude. For sewerage  and sewage disposal
it appears from the Jeger Report[15] that total annual costs lately,
including amortization of capital expenditures (assuming only a
20-year length of life for a sewage works, which is much too small)
would amount to about £100 million, which is consistent with the
figure of £400 million over the last five years referred to by the
then Secretary of State for the Environment, Mr Peter Walker,[16]
since these expenditures have been rising lately to compensate for
a period of severe constraint on the expenditures that local
authorities could incur for this purpose. Thus, although one does
not know what would be an optimum, the fact that the recent
figures have been exceptionally high, plus the fact that the state
of the rivers has improved on the whole over the last decade, suggest that £100 million pa cannot be far short of the optimum at
the present level of GNP. Of course, the demand for water is rising,
but not much faster than GNP.

As regards air pollution, the 105th annual report of the Alkali
Inspectorate provided some figures for industrial air pollution
abatement expenditures for the scheduled industries covered by
the relevant legislation. But is is not clear how far and fast capital
charges have been reduced to an annual basis, and the report points
out that it is difficult to distinguish between genuine anti-pollution
expenditures and installation of new plant, which may be less

polluting than the old plant, but which would have been wholly or partly installed anyway.[17] If the estimates shown therein are doubled to allow for industrial coverage they would amount to about £100 million pa, which is about the same order of magnitude as the water pollution abatement costs, so that, excluding noise and refuse disposal, the cost of reducing water and air pollution would be somewhere about £200 million per annum. Assuming that the levels of abatement implied in these figures are still below optimum and that something substantial must be added for refuse disposal and noise abatement, it is still difficult to come up with an estimate of more than about £500 million,[18] which would be just over 1 per cent of GNP, or about half the best estimate of the USA share. After all, some of the most spectacular improvements in the environment, such as the substantial reduction in smoke pollution in London over the last decade or so, have been achieved at a negligible cost of about 15p per annum (per head of the London population) by comparison with an annual average income per head of several hundred pounds.[19]

Now it may appear surprising that the UK estimates could be half the best estimate for the USA in view of the fact that the population density of the UK is about seven times that of the USA so that the UK does not possess so much free and harmless effluent disposal facilities in the form of sheer space. But against this one must bear in mind that (a) the estimates are subject to such large margins of error that differences of 1 per cent or so of GNP are not significant, (b) the USA has allowed pollution to become far more serious in many cities and rivers than has been the case in the UK, and (c) the targets set out in the estimates by the Council on Environmental Quality are, in many respects, probably beyond the optimum.

It may be that all these estimates are wrong, and anyway they appear to be very deficient from the point of view of the extent to which they correspond to the relevant concept of the total cost to society, current and capital (annual charge) of the optimum programme, given the backlogs and the future rise in needs and so on. Also there is some very fragmentary evidence that suggests that in Canada and in Sweden the corresponding figure might be about 2 per cent of GNP or even more.[20] Nevertheless, even if the correct figure for the UK is as high as 2 per cent, this is still not all that large.

If this is the order of magnitude involved it is not quite worth all the fuss that is being made about it. Failure to devalue the pound earlier in 1967 probably cost the UK much more in terms of lost growth of productive potential than will ever be made up! One to two per cent of GNP is not a great burden, given all the other forms of avoidable sub-optimisation that are constantly experienced, and given also that it could be introduced in stages – unlike a dramatic improvement in the foreign balances.


## POLLUTION AND ECONOMIC GROWTH   *T. P. Hill*

Professor Beckerman has covered much of the ground by reviewing the meaning of any effort to measure the appropriate economic cost of pollution, and also establishing the extent to which any attempt by society to recover the external costs of pollution is likely to affect the prosperity of the country. While I would certainly accept the general conclusions which he reaches, I think some further comment may be helpful on the impact of any attempt by society to recover the costs of pollution from the polluters.

In the first place, it seems necessary to emphasise the extent to which economic growth, unlike population growth, is not capable of objective measurement. Although rapid economic growth is widely accepted as one of the main objectives of economic policy, the extent to which measurement of economic growth may be affected by various non-economic factors is not widely appreciated. The growth of some conventional economic aggregate, such as GNP, is affected by the following factors in particular:

1    The range of human activity which it is decided to include within the scope of the relevant measure.

2    The legal framework within which the economic system operates.

3    The institutional framework within which the economic system operates.

4    A large number of *conventions*, often of a fairly arbitrary nature, which statisticians are obliged to make when compiling comprehensive measures of output and growth. These problems are particularly acute when trying to distinguish changes in prices from changes in volumes for many types of goods and services.

It is not proposed to elaborate on all these points in this paper, but to concentrate on one particular issue: namely, what effect changes in legislation relating to pollution and the environment tend to have on conventional measures of output, growth and productivity.

## The effects of changes in legislation

The legal framework within which the economic system operates is important, primarily because it has a direct bearing on monetary (as distinct from 'real') costs of production. Suppose the law is changed in such a way as to prohibit the discharge of specified wastes into rivers, lakes or the sea. (Changes in legislation of this kind are not, of course, new and have a long history, if we recall periods when it was permitted to throw all kinds of rubbish and filth into the streets – periods when even minimal standards of sanitation and public health were not enforced). The effect of such a prohibition on commercial enterprises will generally be to increase their monetary costs of production as they will have to find means of either eliminating these noxious by-products previously inflicted on the community at large, or effectively disposing of them themselves. Two cases, not necessarily mutually exclusive may be distinguished:

1    the nature of the product is unchanged and only the
method of production is changed

2    the product is changed, because it is itself responsible for
the pollution — the obvious example being the motor car. For
convenience, let us consider the two cases separately.

In the first case, it may be necessary to install some new capital
equipment which, *ceteris paribus*, will cause a temporary rise in
national product, but will also presumably increase current monetary
costs of production (otherwise the profit-maximising entrepreneur
would presumably already be using this method). Given that current
monetary costs per unit of output are increased, either the price of
the product rises, or the profit margin is reduced, or some combination of the two occurs. In general, it may be presumed some price
rise will occur, even if by a smaller proportion than monetary costs
(excluding profits).

Thus, the price of the product will tend to rise relatively to
other products, and there will also be some secondary repercussions
on the prices of products of other industries which utilise the product in question as an input in their own processes of production. It
is difficult to generalise about what the ultimate effects of these
changes would be, as they will depend on purchasers' reactions to
these changes in relative prices.

It is useful to focus attention on the effects of the change in
legislation, *per se*, on the measured aggregates by assuming for
purposes·of argument that (a) all *other* prices, including wage rates
and profit margins, remain constant, except for the prices of those
products which use the product in question as an input into their
own process of production; (b) that the same set of goods and
services as before is to be produced for *final* demand in the form
of consumption or investment.

It can be argued as follows:

1    Although final outputs remain unchanged in real terms
(by assumption), their value will rise in money terms because
of the price increase for the product in question and any

other products using it as an input.

2      The price increase for the product in question is not attributable to increased prices of its own inputs (again by assumption) but to increased quantities of at least some inputs required per unit of output resulting from the changed technique of production.

3      These increased inputs will raise the *total* outputs required from industries which produce them, and hence raise *in real terms* the total outputs required from all industries collectively in order to produce the same initial final outputs.

4      These increases in total outputs will raise the total demand for primary inputs into the system in the form of labour and capital. In this way, the total value of primary incomes generated in the course of production will rise to match the increase in the value of final output in money terms noted under 1 above.

However, it is clear that in real terms the amount of primary inputs required to produce a given final output will have increased. Thus, from an economic point of view productivity will appear to have fallen, but this is merely because various social costs, which previously escaped the accounting framework, will have been translated into monetary costs which enter the circuit of economic transactions.

The point of the example is merely to demonstrate that the measured values of a whole set of economic concepts such as cost, output, and productivity have no independent validity, but are determined by the rules and legal constraints laid down by society itself. Moreover, in this example, it is quite clear that although the aggregate, national product, as conventionally measured will not have increased (again by assumption), the welfare of society will have increased, because certain previously ignored social costs of production will have been fully met in the course of producing the output.

Reverting to case 2 above, in which the product has to be

changed because it is itself responsible for the pollution (for
example, motor vehicles), similar arguments apply. In this case, the
cost of producing the product is evidently increased in real terms,
and assuming the same number of items is produced as before, it
is necessary to examine the effects on conventional economic
measures. In general, it may be assumed that the price per unit of
product will have increased because of the incorporation of anti-
pollution devices. Again, it is also clear that the total real resources,
including primary inputs of labour and capital, absorbed by the
economic system as a whole for the purposes of producing a given
number of units of output will have increased, and thus productivity
both for the industry and the economy as a whole will have fallen.

The interesting question is how the statisticians will decide to
treat the change in the nature of the product itself. There are two
differing schools of thought on this. (a) It can be argued that the
motor car, to take the obvious example, is still a motor car, and in
respect of its basic function of transporting persons, its quality has
not been improved. (b) It can be argued that because it incorporates
new anti-pollution devices, it is a better, ie better quality, motor
car.

In the former case, the increase in price attributable to the
additional costs incurred by the anti-pollution devices will be treated
as a genuine price increase. In the latter case, the modifications will
be treated as leading to a better quality product, and since improvements in quality are equivalent to increases in quantity, no price
increase will be recorded, and the volume of motor car production
will accordingly be increased instead of the average price of cars.
The implication of these two alternative treatments for measures
of price inflation, on the one hand, and real economic growth, on
the other hand, are plain, and they illustrate the importance of
point 4 raised in the introduction to this paper relating to the conventions adopted by statisticians.

## ECONOMIC EFFECTS OF ABATEMENT OF POLLUTION
*J. F. T. Langley*

Two professional economists have given us their own view of the relationship between pollution and production, suggesting that the imposition of appropriate external taxes, or of legal controls over the disposal of effluent, need not represent an impossible burden on the economy as a whole. I should now like to contribute to this disucssion from the point of view of industry itself, because it is one thing to be able to argue that the impact on the national economy is bearable, but another to show that as far as individual industries are concerned, all is well. While not wishing to deny that an industrialist is capable of taking a wide view (even industrialists take no pleasure in fishing in fishless waters or in breathing foul air), we are bound to admit that his principal preoccupation is bound to be with the economic effect of pollution control on his own busine and this means the effect on his own business here and now rather than some distant point in the future.

It is perhaps unfortunate that industrialists are under considerable pressure to take the short view. This is not necessarily of their own wishing. The normal business accounting period is a year, at the end of which the Board has to give an account of its stewardship. There is thus a built-in temptation to maximise profits in the short term and to let the future look after itself. A few — and it is few — more sophisticated companies prepare five-year plans. Even fewer attempt to look further ahead than this. Yet even five years is a short period in terms of the environment.

This tendency to take the short view very often means that in practice expenditure on pollution abatement is deferred as long as possible; when it can no longer be deferred, as little is spent as can be got away with. That this is short-sighted and deplorable is not denied, but people will continue to act in this way until they are convinced of the need to act differently and that it is in their interests to do so. I realise that in saying this I may be accused by my industrial colleagues of showing them up in a bad light, and

giving them less credit than they deserve. This is certainly not my
intention. Of course, there are large numbers of responsible firms
which take a much more enlightened view. The point I am trying
to make is that we have only recently emerged from an era in which
it was assumed (and let us admit from the position of our present
enormous superiority of knowledge it was then not unreasonable
to assume) that the supply of water and the means of disposing of
effluent and other factory emissions were free, or if not free merely
paid for by a part of what was probably regarded as an exorbitant
local government rate. There is thus a psychological impediment to
be overcome. Time and again I have heard expenditure on pollution
described as 'non-productive expenditure'.

It is generally accepted that almost all forms of pollution can be
controlled, if not totally eliminated. The only limiting factor is
money. It is probably right that as a general rule the cost of abatement of pollution should be built into the cost of an article or a
service rather than subsidised out of general taxation, although
there may be a few exceptions to which I shall refer in a moment.
The consumer needs to be educated to an acceptance of this, just
as he now accepts that the cost of an article or a service includes an
element for fair wages, good working conditions, pensions etc.
This should not be too difficult; the climate appears to be right
and public awareness of the pollution is far greater than even a
year ago.

There may be some particularly intractable problems or difficult
geographical areas where government assistance would be justified.
There may also be a case for special assistance in clearing up the
back-log, otherwise the cost to industry may be unduly heavy in the
early years because of past neglect. The CBI has made representations
to government on the subject of investment grants or allowances,
and some improvements were made in the last budget. We believe,
though, that in some industrialised countries investment incentives
in respect of plant for the abatement of pollution are more generous than is the case in the United Kingdom.

Although the concept of building the cost of abatement into the price is sound, there are aspects of it which require examination. If this concept is accepted it means that pollution abatement becomes an element in the system of market competition on which the free enterprise system is based. It is argued that the conscientious firm will be at a cost disadvantage compared with competitors who neglect their environmental responsibilities. There is, of course, something in this, but for three reasons I think its importance tends to be exaggerated. Costs of production do not fall evenly between firms in competition with each other. Some are less well placed than others for access to their markets or to their suppliers. Some provide better working conditions than others or better pensions or better fringe benefits. Always there will be some who are prepared to push out beyond the minimum legal requirement. This is the way progress is made. I think, too, that any disadvantage which the conscientious firm may encounter will be short-run because it will not be long before the laggards are compelled to mend their ways, probably by then at greater cost to themselves. Thirdly, there are signs, particularly in the US, that public opinion is becoming irritated with products which contribute to the pollution of the environment and with industrial processes which do not conform to acceptable standards. It must be said, however, that the argument applies mainly to competing firms within the same country, or in countries of a roughly comparable degree of industrialisation. Other considerations arise in the case of competition from firms in the less developed countries.

I would be more concerned about a different aspect of the question of competitiveness. It is obviously desirable that knowledge of pollution control practices should be shared between firms engaged in the same industry, both nationally and internationally. Such knowledge should be taken out of the realm of trade secrets. To a considerable extent this happens now, very often through the agency of Industrial Research Associations, but so long a the cost of pollution abatement remains an element in competitiveness there will exist a temptation for a company to keep a break-through to itself, particularly as the pressure for even higher standards increases.

It is often argued that because industrial and technological advance has been responsible for causing environmental pollution in the past, the rate of this advance should now be slowed. Subject to one qualification which I will refer to in a moment, industry believes this argument to be unsound.

The control of pollution is expensive and has to be paid for. In our present sate of evolution the wealth-creating process is based on industry and technology. Unless one adopts the extreme view held by some ecologists that the technological society is doomed, the solution to the problem must come from technology. It is argued that because technology in the past has been the cause of pollution, more technology will be the cause of more pollution in the future. This seems to ignore the fact that the problem is now much better understood and that new and improved methods of pollution control are constantly becoming available. It is recognised that it is much easier to build effective anti-pollution devices into new factories than to convert old ones. New investment is therefore needed. I venture to suggest that there are few factories being erected today in the UK in which pollution control has not received adequate attention. In some industries, such as paper and chemicals, anti-pollution measures can account for ten per cent of the total capital cost. On the other hand, to install modern methods of pollution control in old factories is in may cases a near impossibility.

The qualification I referred to is this. Until comparatively recently it was taken for granted that if something could be invented it was right to invent it. We are now much more aware of the need to take fully into account the possible long-term consequences; in other words, we balance the long term risks against the immediate benefits. Unless the long-term risks are very evident, the decision has inclined towards the immediate benefit. This balance of decision may have to change; instead of saying, 'let us proceed because the risks do not seem very great', we are coming to the point of saying, 'until we are as sure as is humanly possible that the long-term risks are negligible, we should not proceed'. In these circumstances we may have to decide not to invent something which could be invented, or to postpone its invention until more is known about its long-term effects.

Where a new process involves a pollution problem, the principle of 'best practicable means' (which principle industry has wholeheartedly supported) may have to be brought into the question. Increasingly we shall find ourself faced with the possibility that 'best practicable means' may not be good enough, in which case we may have to decide not to proceed with a project until means of dealing adequately with its polluting potential have been perfected.

I myself do not believe that this more cautious approach, this emphasis on proof of innocence rather than proof of guilt, is in conflict with industry's belief that the best hope of improving the environment lies in technological innovation and economic growth; a change of emphasis, maybe, but not a change of direction. In the great majority of situations, 'best practicable means' will remain a useful guiding principle.

Economics also has to do with the maximum use of available resources. May I make three pleas on behalf of industry? As we know, the environment has considerable though not infinite capacity to absorb pollutants. Safe limits should be identified. Standards should be fixed at a level no more onerous than is necessary to remain within these safe limits. If, in the interests of perfectionism, standards are fixed unnecessarily high, there is a waste of valuable resources which could be better utilised elsewhere.

Secondly, we need more information about what pollution costs. I emphasise that I am talking of the cost of pollution itself, not of pollution abatement. If we knew more about this, measures which now look prohibitively expensive might be seen to be money well spent in the longer term and our system of priorities might thereby be radically altered. In this connection cost-benefit analysis has a part to play. The Royal Commission's Report, however, was right to point out that this approach has its limitations. As the Report put it, if cost-benefit analysis had been applied to the abolition of slavery, slavery would probably not have been abolished.

Thirdly, on the question of research; this is a plea that since pollution standards are based on research, we should be very sure that the research is thorough and well-founded. The economic effect of precipitate legislation based on inadequate research can be devastating. As far as the UK is concerned, this problem is no doubt well understood, but the preservation of the environment is now an international issue, fraught with emotion almost to the point of hysteria. There is a danger that we may find ourselves under pressure internationally to adopt unrealistic and uneconomic measures based on inadequate or unsound research, to combat threats which on closer examination can be seen to be negligible or non-existent.

### THE UNITED STATES APPROACH TO FISCAL METHODS OF CONTROL AND THE ECONOMIC CONSEQUENCES OF ABATING POLLUTION   *G. MacDonald*

I said earlier that the United States federal authorities believe that, in the long term, the charge system provides a system that can deal efficiently, effectively and equitably with pollution. It provides manufacturers with strong incentives to change production processes and enforce internal management of waste, encourages industry to seek out, and use, new technology rather than argue whether they are feasible or economic. As the cost of pollution control is reflected in prices, producers and consumers of high pollution goods will carry their share of it; and consumers will come to buy goods carrying lower environmental costs.

With the disadvantage of the standard system and the advantaves of the charge system, why hasn't the United States moved more directly into a system of user charges? I think there are several reasons. First, setting of standards and enforcing them seems simple and straightforward, and in line with the way public nuisances are traditionally dealt with. Recognising the substantial advantages in the charge system, we have put proposals to Congress which will be the first of their kind except for charges for sewer systems in the United Kingdom, and I might add that we have a number of examples where, once user charges were established, the rate of polluted effluent went down very rapidly. A meat-processing plant in Kansas City started out with user charges two years ago that ran to about $1,400 per day. Within ninety days the charges were down to $225 per day with a comparable reduction in BOD.

We plan to introduce, if Congress agrees, user charges for lead in gasoline and for $SO_2$. For lead in gasoline we have three processes at work: persuasion, regulation and user charges. In twelve months we were able to persuade the car industry to switch to a low compression engine that would run on 91 octane petrol, which is readily available and lead free. The reasons for switching to lead-free petrol are complex. We see no other way in the near future of controlling emissions to the standards set by Congress for 1975-6 without the use of catalytic elements involving components that would be poisoned by lead. Probably all '75 model vehicles in the USA will carry warranties which will be invalidated if the owners use lead petrol. Amendments to the Clean Air Act gives the Environmental Protection Agency the power to regulate gasoline additives. We propose to make a user charge which will aim at making unleaded gasoline cheaper to the consumer. Details will be worked out in Congress, but the result is expected to be to make unleaded gasoline two cents a gallon cheaper.

To deal with the $SO_2$ problem we propose to make a charge on emissions into the atmosphere which will provide an incentive for $SO_2$ producers to use low sulphur fuels, or to use other means of abatement. The charge would vary with the location of the plant. Plants in areas not meeting primary ambient air standards would be charged twenty cents per pound of sulphur discharged into the atmosphere.

We recognise that the transitional problems will be serious during the next few years. It is likely to cause least harm to employment and output if help is given during the transition to those firms which have a future before them and not to those that do not, and would shortly go under anyway, whether or not pollution control is required of them. One possible form of transitional aid is tax abatement. We do already exempt pollution control equipment from certain sales and use taxes, and many localities make concessions on property taxes. However, I do not look on direct tax as efficient. Much the same can be said of direct grants. We have also considered low cost loans, but they are of little help to firms whose problem is lack of profit, and such loans would compete with other capital needs of government. The way in which government can give most help over transitional problems is in providing retraining for displaced work people.

I would emphasise that pollution control really has a very small economic impact. In the United States in the period 1970-5 the total cost of pollution control for air, water and solid waste will be about $105 billion. This is little less than two per cent of the expected GNP over the same period. I understand that in Japan the corresponding figure has been estimated at four per cent.

Since these gross figures are rather unenlightening, I will give figures for air pollution control costs for a particular industry in 1976, choosing this year because all features of the Air Quality Act will be in force. In the paper industry air pollution control costs in that year will be about $220 million, and this is 0.2 per cent of the value of 1967 shipments and therefore an even smaller proportion of expected shipments in 1976. An idea of what this means is that in industry a five per cent wage increase is the equivalent of 1.1 per cent of the value of total shipments, and thus more than five times as great as the costs of pollution control. This example suggests that my figure of $105 billion for the cost of all pollution control in all industries in 1970-5, while large, is not overwhelmingly large. It should easily be absorbed within economic growth.


## COST-BENEFIT ANALYSIS WHERE CHANGE IS IRREVERSIBLE *A. Young*

In environmental planning there is a distinction between reversible and irreversible decisions; this distinction affects their evaluation in cost-benefit terms. The decision to allow a river to continue to be used as a convenient channel for waste disposal is reversible; it can be re-evaluated at any future date. Tolerating smoke pollution falls into the same category. However, suppose it is decided that the benefits of a particular hill for recreation are outweighed by its value as a source of sand and gravel, and the decision is made to go ahead with quarrying. If at some future date the relative values change, by a fall in the demand for gravel or a rise in that for heath-covered hills, the decision cannot be reversed. The extreme example of irreversible change is the extinction of a biological species. The erection of buildings on rural land, whilst not technologically irreversible, is in present economic and political circumstances virtually so.

The 'conservationist' case is recognised as being far stronger where change is irreversible. However, it can be made to appear less desirable by the application of cost-benefit analysis with cash-flow discounting, ie, the procedure whereby a cost or benefit of B arising in p years hence is assigned a present value of $B\left(\frac{100 - n}{100}\right)^p$ where n is an assumed percentage discount rate.

I suggest that this procedure, devised as a guide to choice between alternative investments, requires modification when applied to conservation decisions.

My argument is that in cost-benefit analysis, *where change is permanent, cash-flow discounting is inappropriate.* The benefits from conservational measures extend over a long period of time. Yet if discounted at, say, 5 per cent, any benefit derived more than 50 years hence has a negligible present value; even over 20 years the present value is less than 4 per cent of its value at the future date. Suppose the threatened hill referred to above has a value to me alone of £10 per year; if I live for 20 years, its value to me in the twentieth year is the same as its value this year, ie £10, not £10 x $(0.95)^{20}$. I may die, but the hill will have the same value to my children. By extension, insofar as we have an obligation to unborn generations, the appropriate discount rate is nil.

Therefore in assessing the benefits of an environmental resource in danger of being destroyed I suggest the following procedure:

1    Assess its annual value
2    Multiply this by the number of years over which it is
     reasonable to assume the continuance of present society and
     conceptual values.

The latter figure might reasonably be taken, according to one's predilections, at somewhere between 50 and 500 years. I suggest 200 years would be an appropriate working figure.


## COST-BENEFIT ANALYSIS – FURTHER REMARKS
*W. Beckerman*

One of the points made in my main written statement was that charges or taxes on polluters which should be related to the amount of pollution they do or some proxy variable, are a more economical means of achieving any desired reduction in pollution than direct controls or regulations. I do not wish to add to the arguments set out in that paper, except perhaps to say that there is no difference between charges and direct controls with respect to the amount of data needed in order to arrive at a decision as to what is the optimum amount of pollution abatement. Thus, it is not a criticisim of the charges approach to say that we do not have the data required to fix the perfect 'optimum' charge. Exactly the same data limitations apply in deciding on a quantitative control. The point is that, given the available weaknesses of the data, one has to make a decision about the optimum amount of pollution abatement. Once that decision has been reached, there is no difference between charges and controls with respect to practical difficulties of implementation or difficulties arising out of imperfect knowledge.

I would like here to raise a rather different point which has a bearing on the choice between charges, on the one hand, and some form of payment or compensation to polluters to reduce their pollution, on the other hand. In this connection I would like to emphasise the symmetry between charges and subsidies: both are simply transfer payments related to some variable, such as the amount of pollution produced, the only difference being the direction in which the transfer payment flows. This symmetry corresponds to a symmetry between the 'bad', namely the pollution, and the 'good', namely the unpolluted environment. For example, more dirty water in a stream simply means less clean water in a stream. If one thinks that there is too much effluent in a stream one can either tax the 'bad' or subsidise the 'good' (the clean water). Both measures have the same effect. From the point of view of the resource allocation, therefore, it makes no difference which one is applied. But it does make a big difference to income distribution and may offend some people's sense of equity.

At the same time, governments frequently adopt policy measures which take the form of removing a subsidy which some section of the community had hitherto enjoyed but taking accompanying measures to soften the blow. Since the removal of the subsidy is exactly symmetrical to the imposition of a tax, one should not rule out, as a matter of principle, the possibility that in imposing a tax on a polluter a government might want to take accompanying measures to soften the blow. For example, it is often recognised that import duties are undesirable from a resource allocation point of view and, in consultation with other countries, these are occasionally reduced. The removal of an import duty is exactly analogous to the removal of a subsidy previously enjoyed by the protected domestic industries. In such cases, however, it is generally recognised that some sort of transition period has to be allowed in order to give the domestic factors of production adequate time to adjust to the situation. It is for this reason that transitional periods are invariably built into any tariff reduction negotiations. Hence, there would be nothing in principle new about allowing polluters some transition period when introducing some charge or tax on the amount of their pollution. In any case, similar arrangements are made when direct controls on their permitted pollution are imposed.

In certain cases it may even be thought so inequitable to impose a pollution tax on a polluter that it would be preferable to pay the polluter a certain amount per unit of his pollution abatement. In other words, this would amount to a compensation to the polluter for the loss of profits he will have to incur in reducing his pollution. This looks like an ordinary subsidy and it has sometimes been objected that this would impose a distortion which would contravene rules of good conduct in international trade. But this is a misconception. A payment to a polluter per unit of his pollution abatement is not a subsidy to his output since it does not lower his cost curve at all. In fact, his supply curve will be raised in exactly the same way as if he were taxed for his pollution. Such compensation payment is, in effect, an indirect tax on the pollution matched by a 'lump sum' subsidy to the polluter to compensate him for the loss of profits involved in his paying the tax.

Thus, considerations of equity no more constitute an insuperable obstacle to some use of the price mechanism to achieve the optimum degree of pollution abatement than do considerations of data imperfections or administrative inconvenience. Equity consideration can be handled by the price mechanism in the same way as they already are in other areas of economic policy, such as the tariff reduction case mentioned above. The reasons why it is cheaper, from the national point of view and also from the point of view of any given industry, to achieve the optimum degree of pollution abatement by means of taxes or charges rather than direct control, have been set out in my original written statement, so I need not

repeat them here. Some interesting empirical work in the USA has
demonstrated that, in practice, very great economies are obtained
if some sort of charging system is used to abate pollution rather
than direct control.[23] I have pointed out that in order to arrive at
a decision on the desired degree of pollution abatement by direct
control the data imperfections are as much a hindrance as they are
to decisions which are to be implemented by means of charges.*

*Cost-Benefit Analysis and the Middle Class View of Pollution*
I agree, of course, with many of the points made by preceding
speakers concerning the difficulties of measuring adequately the
various items which should, in principle, enter into a cost-benefit
analysis. But this phenomenon of measurement difficulty is one
which has been experienced by all sciences since the beginning of
time. Physicists now measure many concepts which in the more
distant past were thought to be virtually unmeasurable. Thus,
measurement difficulties must never be a reason for abandoning
the conceptually valid methods of appraisal. In any case, considerable progress has already been made over the last few years in
techniques of measurement for many of the items which have to
enter into a cost analysis. Conceptual and theoretical problems
which had not been faced a few years ago, simply because there
was no need to do so, have now been solved in the economics
literature, and, although the resources devoted to this sort of work
have been negligible by comparison with the amount of resources
put into scientific research on pollution problems, considerable
progress has been made in many areas and will no doubt continue
to be made.
Meanwhile, even rough estimates of a theoretically relevant

* Mr F E Ireland did not accept this view, arguing that industry should not
be allowed to set its own level of emission by paying for it. The control
authorities should decide what standards of emission and dispersion they will
permit and then ensure that these standards are implemented by effective
inspection.

variable provide a salutory check to decisions which might, other-wise, be based on the pure self-interest of a few parties concerned in the decision-making process. For example, it is not difficult to find instances where local authorities might be prepared to spend millions of .pounds on some river purification scheme (aided by expensive drainage installations) largely under the influence of the preferences of the middle-class sections of the community who attach considerable importance to their fishing and boating interests. It might be preferable, in such cases, to spend the money on improving local housing conditions, hospitals, schools, etc.

The advantage of a cost-benefit analysis exercise is that it does force the decision makers to recognise that the costs involved in reducing pollution represent resources which could have been used for adding to community facilities in other ways so that, if they are to be used for pollution abatement, it is incumbent on them to be absolutely sure that the social value of the corresponding pollution abatement does exceed the cost of the resources used. Of course, these cost-benefit analyses should not exclude any item of cost or benefit whatsoever, material or 'immaterial'. Many non-economists are under the impression that the economist is only concerned with 'material' benefits, and consequently is not inter-ested in the amenity benefits from pollution abatement. This could not be further from the truth. Economics is the science of the allocation of resources between competing ends, irrespective of whether those ends are material, spiritual, intangible, aesthetic or any other form of end.

## DISCUSSION
There was general agreement that the maximum abatement of pollution is not necessarily the optimum, and that ideally pollution should be so controlled as to equate the environmental benefit with the cost of abatement in greater consumption of resources or lower output of goods and services. Doubts was expressed, however,

about the practical application of this principle. In particular, Mr
Ireland argued for retaining, where control of industrial pollution
of the air is concerned, the doctrine of requiring the use of the
'best practicable means' of abatement. This was interpreted by the
courts in the United Kingdom as meaning the best means that are
reasonably practicable economically. Application of this doctrine,
which was well tried and well understood, and fairly inexpensive
to administer, produced in practice much the same results as would
be produced by a system which used fiscal means (taxation for
emitting pollution or subsidy for abating it) to achieve the theoretical optimum.

Mr Price said that Professor Beckerman had drawn a useful
universal diagram, (Figure 15) with which it was possible, in many
instances, to illustrate the economic issues underlying the allocation
of resources for social purposes. However, it was important to
appreciate that social and monetary costs at the margin — which
the diagram compared — are not necessarily measurable in the same
units: the diagram ceased to be of practical use unless some conversion
factor could be identified and generally agreed upon. In reality the
conversion factor was often extremely arbitrary. Depending on the
shape of the curves, or on who did the analysis, factors of three
could quite easily be introduced either way; and the so-called
'optimal point' could be made to move wildly around the diagram.
In other words, although the diagram was useful in a way of
looking at a problem, the concept of an identifiable and universally
acceptable optimum was unlikely to find general approval. As an
illustration one might imagine that some measure in the field of
public health would add one day to the average life expectancy of
the people in this country. Then, if the time gained were valued
at the average per-capita income, the benefit would be around
£15 million per day. But another analyst could quite easily argue
that, since people whose lives would be extended would be at the
end of their lives, their value to the community would effectively
be zero, or even negative. At all events, there would be a different

figure. The Ministry of Transport had run into similar problems in trying to find ways of controlling congestion in the streets of London. In theory this can be done with electronic road pricing; but one of the reasons why nobody has actually adopted this method was that before it can be introduced a down payment has to be made in hard cash. In return the social benefits might be perhaps a few minutes saved per commuter day; and what that is worth to the community is extremely debatable. He would add that the way in which controls were imposed was all-important, particularly their phasing. At an earlier conference at the University of East Anglia an account had been given of the catastrophic disruption which the ban on the use of cyclamates had created in the British soft drinks industry. In considering how to encourage industrialists to introduce anti-pollution measures, it was important to realise that industry (at any rate in the United Kingdom) had a very short time-horizon for planning; and money today was regarded as worth much more than money in three years' time. If, therefore, it was the aim to encourage industry to reduce pollution through the persuasive effect of fiscal measures, it would be better to rely on direct grants than on taxation allowances, which would take three to four years to work through the system.

Mr Chilver adverted to what had been said about the consequences of pollution control on national economies. He submitted that there were unsatisfied claims on national resources which were at least as urgent as abating pollution, such as housing, house-improvement and education. Several million people were still living in houses without indoor sanitation. Bad housing must account for much more ill-health than any form of environmental pollution. No doubt there were many ways in which resources were being used in this country on unnecessary personal consumption, and if all resources were deployed to the best advantage the country could spend much more, both on social services, and on improving the environment. In practice, however, the ability of a democratic government to direct resources to particular ends is limited. Most of the money raised in taxation is hypothecated already. (It was relevant here that the unit price of what the state spends money on, which is largely services or goods with a high labour content, tends to go up in real terms at the same pace as the real increase in the GNP). It was said of many things that people advocated that their cost was 'only' one per cent of the GNP, but the total that the government could divert to new forms of expenditure at any one time was not much greater than that. Where the government exercises the closest control, ie in public spending, the years since the war had seen a cyclical process in which expenditure rose for a few years and was then abruptly cut back for economic reasons. When people said that they were willing to see increases in the price of commodities resulting from heavier expenditure on preventing pollution during manufacture, there was sometimes the unspoken assumption that personal spending power would nevertheless continue to rise in real terms. Large sections of the community were able to ensure that, so far as their own incomes were concerned, this in fact came about. So, abating pollution did compete with other desirable objectives. It was bearing this in mind in applauding, for example, heavy expenditure that results in the reappearance of coarse fish in certain rivers. And while it would clearly be wrong to advocate that economic growth should be pursued regardless of the consequences, economic growth increased the country's ability to allot resources to improving the environment.

Mr Chilver went on to express agreement with Professor Beckerman's theses that (1) the objective of governments in controlling pollution should be to reduce its disbenefits in harm to health and amenity to an extent that was neither greater nor less than the disbenefits of pollution abatement in higher costs and loss of production; and (2) the logical way to do so was to use fiscal means, such as tax on emissions calculated to equal the cost of the emissions to the community. However, he saw considerable practical difficulties in applying these principles in all fields, or even in the minority of them. As to the *calculation of costs and benefits*, a common difficulty was that scientific knowledge was inadequate to enable even the most tentative estimates to be made of the physical or biological effects of a particular measure of control. The variables were too numerous. This had been brought out in the papers about scientific input (Chapter 2 above). Another difficulty comparing costs and benefits was the familiar one of assessing harm to amenity in the same medium as economic disbenefits. Techniques had been proposed for doing this; for example, estimating the value of a piece of scenery from the costs incurred by people in going to look at it. However, these techniques did not eliminate the essentially subjective nature of the values involved: many people would strongly deny that the spiritual value of a piece of scenery could be equated with the time and expense that average members of the population incurred in visiting it. Decisions by central or local government where subjective values were balanced against objective ones would always in practice be political ones. A technique that would help such processes would, he suggested, be for the Minister or other authority to prepare a costed list of possible improvements to amenity: the subjective value of conserving amenity in a particular case could then be compared with other items *in pari materia*. He hoped that this technique would come to be employed. However, it would not eliminate the essentially political nature of decisions containing a subjective element. It was instructive that the decision about the location of the third London Airport had wholly set aside the result of the most elaborate exercise in cost-benefit analysis ever carried out in this country. Where the difficulties of estimating costs and benefits in the same medium could be overcome, the *fiscal methods of control* advocated by Professor Beckerman had considerable attraction. They had proved themselves in practice in this country in that charges by a local authority for receiving an industrial element were often based on the cost of treating it; and charges for abstracting water were based on supply and demand in the locality in question, and the cost of increasing supply, and on the quality of the water before and after abstraction. There was probably scope for greater use of fiscal methods of control. However, they would probably be more expensive administratively in some instances. Moreover, they were normally unacceptable politically for the control of pollution liable to endanger public health or safety.

Notes to this chapter are on page 196

# 4: Government Processes in Determining and Applying Controls

This chapter opens with a short resume by Dr Holdgate[1] of the general considerations bearing on the way government authorities should reach decisions about standards, etc and the forms controls should take. This is followed by examinations by Professor Cole, Mr Ireland and Mr Lippitt of practice in the United Kingdom in protection of water, air and land respectively. Dr MacDonald then describes current practice in the United States, with special reference to participation of the public in decision-making. The ensuing discussion showed no major disagreement with the lines on which practice in the two countries has been developing, though reservations were expressed on particular points.

**THE MECHANICS OF POLLUTION CONTROL**  *M. W. Holdgate*
   The diagram (Fig 16) summarises the relationships between environmental quality standards or goals and the other kinds of derivèd working level that may appear in each area – land, fresh water, sea – and considers their relative importance. I think it is important to recall that many environmental quality, or ambient, 'standards' have been no more than goals people have sought to attain in the environment, and that emission standards, codes of practice, and product standards are the devices used to attain them. As operational devices they stand aside from fiscal mechanisms of

## FRESHWATER

**EMISSION STANDARDS**
(outfalls etc.)

**CODES OF PRACTICE**
(sewage treatment etc.)

**PRODUCT STANDARDS**
(e.g. boat sanitation)

Environmental quality standards OR goals

_at source or treatment works or point of release_

## SEA

**CODES OF PRACTICE**
Dumping
(ship e.g. tanker operators)

**EMISSION STANDARDS**
(outfalls)

**PRODUCT STANDARDS**
(ship design)

Environmental quality standards OR goals

_at point of release to environment_

## AIR

**EMISSION STANDARDS**

**CODES OF PRACTICE**
(plant operations)

**PRODUCT STANDARDS**
(e.g. vehicles)

Environmental quality standards OR goals

_all at source of pollution_

## LAND

**CODES OF PRACTICE**
(e.g. pesticides, refuse disposal)

_at source or final injection to environment_

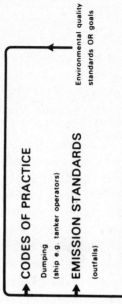
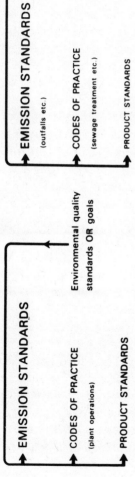

taxation, subsidy, or direct charging, which we also use to tilt the balance in one direction or another.

For air, the direct control of emissions at source is probably best, but there is an important role for codes of operational practice; and in vehicles we know that product standards are useful. Some governments have set environmental quality 'goals'. For land, I am not aware that anyone has tried to set environmental quality standards as such, and most of the land pollution control measures I know of are codes of practice, as for pesticide application, or refuse disposal. These codes can operate at source, governing how the pesticide is made or tested before being marketed, or at the point of injection to the environment as a crop spray or as a refuse dump. For fresh water, environmental quality standards have been set, and I agree that they can be valuable, especially if they are varied pragmatically, reach by reach, river by river, area by area, lake by lake. But all the same, the control of emissions to fresh water at individual outfalls must remain the primary means of control, together with codes of practice, for example, for treating sewage. There are also some product standards, eg for boat sanitation on the Norfolk Broads. One may thus control either at the source, or at the point of release into the environment. At sea there can also be guiding goals of environmental quality, but in practical terms the real action depends particularly on codes of practice, for example, for controlling dumping, or for reducing oil pollution. However, emission standards for direct discharges via outfalls are also important, as are product standards in ship design.

Of course, all these interconnect. For example, pesticides sprayed on crops from aircraft do not all reach their targets, and may reach the sea through the air or via rivers. The control of that kind of marine pollution can only occur back at source, by good codes of practice for application of the pesticides to the land. As a final and sweeping generalisation, I would guess that environmental quality standards are most useful 1) when one is dealing with fairly discrete sections of the environment like a lake, where one can quantify the dilution capacity, the inflow and outflow, the relationship between the input, concentration in the environment, and so on rather easily; or 2) if the environmental quality stan-standards are being set by centralised strategic bodies not themselves directly responsible for translating the standards into codes of practice. If one is, for example, a federal agency or a regional agency with a large area to cover, one may try to set general goals for quality of the environment which it becomes the business of those actually operating pollution control to translate into practical action, through devising and enforcing emission controls or codes of practice. It may be that Dr MacDonald's position and ours differ slightly, because he belongs to a federal agency with a very large area to consider but without direct responsibility on the ground, whereas we tend, in a small country, to go more directly and easily to the points of application.

## GOVERNMENTAL ACTION IN THE UNITED KINGDOM FOR THE PROTECTION OF WATER  *H. A. Cole*

It will be convenient to consider amenities and resources under three zonal sub-heads: 1. Rivers; 2. Estuaries and coastal waters; 3. Offshore waters

The division between zones 2 and 3 lies at the boundary of territorial waters as generally agreed. Questions relating to the terrestrial environment are not considered. Comments refer to conditions in the United Kingdom.

Further sub-division of amenity and resources may be achieved as follows:

1 *Rivers*

Resource aspects    a   potable water

b   water for industrial purposes

c   commercial fisheries

     (1)   salmon and trout (2) coarse fish

d   waste disposal

                 e  transport

Amenity aspects      a  visual appearance and landscape value

                 b  recreational fishing

                 c  boating

                 d  bathing

                 e  nature conservation

2 *Estuaries and coastal waters*

Resource aspects     a  Industrial purposes, especially power production

                 b  fisheries

                     (1) salmon and trout (2) shellfish (3) seafish

                 c  transport

                 d  waste disposal

                 e  mineral extraction, especially gravel

                 f  desalination

                 g  defence

Amenity aspects      a  Visual appearance and landscape value

                 b  bathing

                 c  boating

                 d  nature conservation

                     (1) seabirds (2) seals and other mammals (3) areas of special interest

3 *Offshore waters*

Resource aspects     a  fisheries

                 b  transport

                 c  mineral extraction, especially gas and oil

                 d  nature conservation

                     (1) seabirds (2) seals and other mammals

This classification is intended to focus attention on the different purposes for which 'environmental standards' may be required and to suggest possible areas of conflict. The limiting factors in the three zones are not the same, and moreover within zones nothing approaching uniformity of treatment has been achieved or is likely

to be possible. For example, among the different English rivers
some, such as the Test and the Hampshire Avon, are considered
primarily as major centres of salmon and trout fishing, and pollution
standards are set so as to maintain these in a productive condition.
Others are considered primarily as sources of potable water, while
a few seem to be regarded mainly as channels for conveying sewage
and industrial waste to the sea. Within a single river system the
primary use may change drastically from the headwaters (potable
water and tourism), down to the lower reaches (waste disposal).
Similarly, some areas of coastal water are of unique value for
fisheries (eg shellfish production or as fish spawning grounds), while
in others the interests of seaborne traffic, defence or recreation may
be paramount. Only in offshore waters is the problem a fairly
simple one with little serious conflict between users.

The following notes are intended to pinpoint some of the
pollution problems of importance in the three zones considered
above. They are by no means comprehensive and are offered merely
as guide lines for the discussion.

*Rivers*

In many rivers, particularly in the east and south of England,
water requirements for domestic and industrial use tend to become
dominant to the detriment of other considerations, particularly
visual appearance and fisheries. Exceptions are provided by rivers
which carry salmon and trout fisheries, as these are now very
valuable and their owners are capable of exerting a powerful influence. Upland rivers in tourist areas tend to become areas of
conflict with water suppliers and, unless public opinion is actively
mobilised on a local basis — as, for example, in the Lake District —
some deterioration in their amenity value is probable;

Pollution standards for potable and industrial waters are generally
less stringent than for the maintenance of fisheries, and certainly
less exacting than are required to maintain a fully satisfactory
visual appearance and maximum landscape value. Recreational

fishing generally, and especially the very large number who angle for coarse fish, would benefit substantially from higher standards in rivers.

There are sharp conflicts between the use of rivers for waste disposal and almost all other interests except, perhaps, transport, but that is now relatively unimportant above tidal reaches.

Important categories of pollutants are sewage; other organic wastes with a high oxygen demand; toxic materials of all kinds, especially cyanides, chlorinated hydrocarbons, heavy metal compounds and metalloids. In addition to toxicity, major problems arise from turbity, discoloration, excess nutrients, scums, oil and foaming.

## Estuaries

These are the area of maximum conflict of interests. The major industrial use of water is for cooling, especially in power stations, and nuclear installations may require very large quantities daily. Desalination is, however, beginning to become a commercial proposition and may be more important in the future. There are fisheries of major importance in estuaries for salmon and sea trout; other estuarine species such as smelts are now rare. Shellfish beds, eg mussels and cockles, are common. Sea transport is extremely important, also recreational boating. Carriage of wastes to the sea is a major use which is still increasing despite the development of coastal pipelines for industrial waste and trunk sewers discharging on the open coast.

All the major categories of pollutants create serious local problems, eg deoxygenation, toxicity, contamination of seafoods with pathogens and metallic residues, fouling of beaches with oils, scums and non-degradable plastics.

In estuaries pollution standards tend to be low, unless there are highly productive shellfish beds (oysters, mussels and clams). Even the existence of important salmon fisheries does not impose high standards because fish may pass through heavily polluted waters during periods of flood and maximum tidal dilution. Where bathing is practicable, higher standards may be demanded, but banning of stretches for bathing or shellfish cultivation may be considered to be an acceptable alternative to treatment of sewage and industrial wastes. Heavy pollution of estuaries has come to be accepted as the norm and their former importance for fish and shellfish production has been forgotten. Sailing, as an alternative use of the sheltered waters, does not demand a high environmental standard.

The most damaging categories of pollutants are sewage and organic wastes with a high oxygen demand and much material in suspension, and toxic and persistent wastes of all kinds. Oil and chemicals liable to taint shellfish (such as phenols) are highly objectionable. Bulky inert wastes liable to cause turbidity and discoloration very greatly reduce amenities. Non-degradable plastics are a serious problem. Persistent hydrocarbons and metals may accumulate in fish and shellfish.

*Coastal Waters*

As one moves from estuaries to open coastal waters, recreational use, especially for bathing, becomes particularly important. All forms of boating and marine transport reach maximum intensity, while sea fisheries, especially those for molluscs, crustacea, herring and sprat, assume greater importance.

In coastal waters the problems and conflicts are similar to those in estuaries but are generally less severe because of more rapid dispersal and dilution of pollutants. Public health protection from sewage contamination on beaches demands, generally speaking, less stringent standards than those needed for shell fish production because the molluscs may accumulate pathogenic organisms. The presence of traces of persistent chlorinated hydrocarbons and heavy metals may cause no concern except because of possible effects on fisheries which may be damaged directly or may become unmarketable.

There are serious conflicts in coastal waters between those

seeking cheap disposal of sewage and industrial wastes from coastal conurbations, and the protection of fisheries and maintenance of amenities. A slow deterioration has been evident in recent years. The most important pollutants are sewage, because of contained pathogens; bulky organic wastes, because of high oxygen demand and effects on amenities; persistent and toxic materials of all kinds and, especially, oil. The latter provides the overriding amenity problem and very substantial expenditure is entailed annually in keeping it under control. Seabird destruction is a serious and continuing problem. Excessive addition of nutrients from sewage is beginning to cause concern.

## Offshore Waters

The pollution aspects which need to be considered are the widespread dissemination of highly persistent and toxic materials, such as chlorinated hydrocarbons and heavy metals, especially those distributed through the air, and the dumping of wastes from ships, especially anything which may obstruct fishing. Oil at sea is a menace to seabirds wherever it occurs but is not damaging to fisheries. Environmental standards, if adopted, need to be considered on a global scale.

## GOVERNMENTAL ACTION IN THE UNITED KINGDOM FOR THE PROTECTION OF THE AIR   *F. E. Ireland*

If I ask Professor Lawther and Dr Pochin 'Can the public tolerate x microgrammes per cubic metre of a certain pollutant?' they can say 'Yes, that is all right', but they cannot tell me precisely where the threshold is. There seems to be a tremendous range of physiological responses. For discussion of some of these points, see chapter 2: 'Air Pollution and its Effects on Man' by Professor Lawther.

Many emission standards are set in the United Kingdom under the Alkali Act. There are two basic requirements. First of all, the best practicable means shall be used to prevent the emission of noxious or offensive gases. Second, all such necessarily discharged gases shall be rendered harmless and inoffensive. Because 100 per cent prevention of a discharge cannot be achieved, some residual gases are left, and there are sometimes no known means of preventing emission of offensive products of combustion. One of the favourite yardsticks for pollution from combustion is sulphur dioxide. When it is so used, it is important to recognise that it is no more than a yardstick for a whole host of pollutants. When you burn coal you produce oxides of nitrogen which can be highly toxic. There are also lead, fluorides, mercury, beryllium and radioactive substances. You could find anything you care to mention in emissions from the burning of coal. Many other industrial emissions are composed of a mixture of gases.

We believe that control should be based on standards of prevention. How far is it possible to go along the road to perfection? If money were no object, we could get very near to perfection. But money is an object, and economics must enter into this word 'practicable'. It must be technically *and* economically practicable to prevent. Having done what we can to prevent, we come to the second part, which is rendering the remaining emissions harmless and inoffensive. There are no definitions of what is harmless and inoffensive, because what could be harmless and inoffensive to one person may not be so to another who has certain weaknesses or allergies. We just cannot protect all the public all the time.

Tall chimneys are used for dispersing waste gases in the air and rendering them harmless and inoffensive. There are many formulae for dispersion of pollutants, and these have the backing of many authorities. Unfortunately they do not all give the same answer, and even a single formula can lead to several widely varying answers depending on the parameters used, such as a parameter for maximum ground level concentration of pollutant. Changes in the weather can cause a variation of twentyfold in environmental concentrations. Also, no pollutant exists in isolation, and it is probably unusual for a pollutant to act in a specific manner unrelated to the effects of other pollutants. Radioactivity is one whose actions on humans can be dealt with in isolation, but most emissions, particularly those involving the combustion of fuels or heating of minerals are mixtures of pollutants. This is why it is common practice to choose the most significant substance, such as sulphur dioxide, for use as a yardstick.

With all this in mind, it is obvious that choosing the right chimney height is as much a matter of experience as mathematics. The inspectorate has a long experience of trial and error, and, since 1935, of the mathematical approach. Rules have been developed to combine the two to suit meteorological conditions in Britain, and the monitoring evidence is that acceptable environmental conditions ensue.

A factor to be taken into account over chimney heights is the effect of breakdowns of the plant. The chimney can act as a safety valve. Equipped with a tall chimney, a works can sometimes keep operating when arrestment plant has suffered a breakdown, whereas with a chimney meeting no more than the minimum requirement the effect at ground level would be intolerable.

The inspectorate can frequently persuade firms to look into the future and install chimneys to take account of forseeable future expansion. This is particularly relevant to oil refineries.

It is the inspectorate's normal practice to set uniform national standards of emission, and to vary the heights of chimneys for dispersion to take account of local circumstances. Flexibility is always left for local inspectors to adjust their requirements to deal with special circumstances.

For industry as a whole, standards of emission are usually arrived at only after close discussion with both individual firms and trade associations, taking into account the technical possibilities, costs, and current information on the effects of pollutants on human and animal health, vegetation and odour thresholds. Standards of emission are continually being made tougher as technology

advances, or as works become larger and so able to achieve a greater
degree of prevention at economic cost than a small works.

There are many industrial processes for which standards of
emission cannot be set or would be difficult to implement. Emissions
can result from failure of equipment or from leaks and from
materials being handled or in store. It is then necessary to apply the
'best practicable means' criterion to the use of techniques of prevention and planned maintenance. Often important decisions face the
designer and inspector on the duplication of pumps or fans, or the
choice between using cheap, easily replaceable materials of construction or expensive materials able to withstand erosion. The
consequences of failure have to be taken into account. A runaway
reaction or operational abnormality can overload the arrestment
plant, or the arrestment plant itself may suffer a breakdown; either
can lead to excessive emissions of pollutants. If these pollutants
are inert and merely lead to a temporary deterioration of local
amenities, the effect is not serious, but incidents leading to the
escape of highly toxic or offensive materials, such as hydrogen
cyanide, chlorine, mercaptans or radioactives, might be highly
dangerous or unacceptable. In the latter cases, it is necessary to
take such precautions as providing extra arrestment plants in series
or parallel, or abnormally large absorber capacity, so that, when a
breakdown occurs in a unit, the remainder can still contain the
emission adequately. Where the consequences of a failure are
exceptionally serious, normal emissions may be only a small
fraction of any scientifically based standard. For example, radioactive emissions from Harwell are only about 1 per cent of 'derived
working limits' based on ICRP recommendations. In such cases any
significant emission above normal is a danger signal to be taken
seriously.

The first thing we must do in looking at the dispersion of
emissions is to ensure that there is no obvious public health hazard.
What is important in estimating a public health hazard? Is it a
sudden high concentration over a short period, or is it a long-term

concentration over a period of years? These are complicated questions. In the absence of the scientific knowledge to answer them adequately, we play for safety and aim at a very small fraction of what the factory inspector would allow in a factory atmosphere. You may know that the factory inspectorate have adopted the United States Conference of Hygenists' list of what is allowable in a factory atmosphere. For an instantaneous concentration at ground level we aim at approximately one-thirtieth of what the factory inspector would allow. The operator only works for eight hours a day, but the householder might be exposed for twenty-four. Taking account also of the assumed lesser resistance of the aged, the infirm and the young, we arrive at this factor of one-thirtieth. The permissible concentration that we arrive at in this way is usually about $1 - 0.3^0/_{00}$ of the chimney concentration. It is not the mass emission from chimneys that counts so much as their effect at ground level, a point which is often missed. The largest power station being built in this country will emit about 1,200 tons of sulphur dioxide a day. From past experience of power stations we estimate the contributions such a power station will make to the background concentration in a rural area will be about 4 per cent, an amount barely measurable.

Although we safeguard public health in this way, I think that almost every piece of legislation about air pollution in this country has been directed to protecting amenity rather than health. From the first Alkali Act of 1863 (which was based on the scorching of the surrounding areas by hydrochloric acid from alkali works) onwards, public health has been regarded as an inadequate basis for legislation because of the difficulty of proving that a danger to health exists. Even going back a hundred years, statistics showed that the health of people in the industrial areas of Lancashire and in Glasgow was at least as good as that of those living in Harrogate and Brighton. The one possible exception to this is the Clean Air Act of 1956. This followed the 1952 London smog which caused the deaths of 4,000 people; but public pressure for control of

smoke in the interests of amenity would no doubt have brought
it about in any case. Most of our decisions in setting standards
have been based on pragmatic assessment of amenity. We try to
disperse emissions to the point where, when they get back to
ground level, they will be unnoticeable. On the other hand, we try
to eliminate odours from hydrogen sulphide by excluding it from
industrial processes rather than by relying on dispersal. We have
not achieved perfection in our efforts to do so.

The Alkali Inspectorate provides this country's representatives
at discussions about clean air arranged by OECD, the Council of
Europe, NATO, UNESCO, EEC, and many other international
organisations. (I may say that there is considerable overlapping
between these discussions, with a consequent waste of time).
Representatives of the United States at these discussions initially
advocated the use of air quality criteria as a method of control.
There are clearly attractions in this, but there are practical difficulties in applying it. To which firms do you say 'You shut down' or
'You change to a low sulphur fuel' in order to achieve a specified
level of air quality in a complex of a thousand industrial installations?
In this country we have preferred to proceed by minimising each
source. Although it is representatives of the federal government of
the United States who attend meetings of international organisations, it is the states and the cities of America who exercise control,
and they have in practice proceeded in the same way as we in this
country. The 1967 Air Quality Act in America gave the federal
government power to define regional air resource management
areas and to seek to get air quality criteria applied in them; but in
December 1970 the United States introduced new legislation
setting national source standards. I would like to quote you the
introduction to an article by Victor Sussman, Director of the
Pennsylvania Department of Environmental Resources, in April
1971.

> Recent federal air pollution control laws and regulations have
> required significant changes in the plan for developing regulations to

limit emissions and achieve acceptable air quality. Major elements of the so-called 'air resources management concept' have been found in practice to be meaningless and/or unworkable. Experience in designating air quality control in regions, interpreting air quality criteria and adopting ambient and emission standards have indicated a need to change our approach and discontinue a number of past non-productive activities. The Clean Air Amendment of 1970 called for a more direct and pragmatic approach, for example, basing emission standards on the best available control technology. It is now necessary to overcome the momentum built up in attempting to implement the now obsolete elements of the Air Quality Act of 1967. Present efforts and concern for the air quality control regions' exotic diffusion modelling and extensive criteria development should be replaced with efforts to develop practicable and effective emission standards, enforcement techniques and land use standards.

So you see that Americans are changing to the same kind of methods as we use here. I do not discount air quality criteria as goals for the future. I think they can be valuable, so long as they are treated as *goals* and not as standards or means of control emission.

More important than the setting of standards is their implementation. There has recently been in effect competition between countries in setting the most exacting standards. The Iron Curtain countries, some of the states in the United States, and more recently some European countries are setting standards which, I believe, are virtually impossible to enforce.

## GOVERNMENTAL ACTION IN THE UNITED KINGDOM FOR THE PROTECTION OF LAND  *A. J. Lippitt*

I am concerned with the problem of mineral extraction in relation to the other competing uses of land. There are various factors which make it difficult to apply standards in this field, factors such as taste (one man's amenity is another man's pollution), and the extent of the need for towns and cities

to expand into the countryside, so as to provide houses for people
who are at present living in poor conditions. There are questions
of 'changeover times', a situation of environmental pollution that,
for example, Professor Cole may worry about in relation to his
estuaries or rivers, but that also affects mineral extraction. Our
'pollutant' can become an amenity in, say, twenty or thirty years'
time when a flooded gravel pit becomes a source for fishing or
available for recreation, and therefore an amenity.

Although a great deal of the discussion on mineral extraction
is in relation to the less common minerals which exist in this
country, such as copper in Snowdonia, there is the more
serious problem relating to the construction materials with which
this university is built — stone, sand and gravel. The problems
there arise because there is no alternative means whereby we can
get these basic aggregate minerals for the construction industry.
We use approximately 200 million tons per annum, and on current
assumptions about economic growth and usage we shall use
more than 1,000 million tons per annum by the end of the
century. This is equivalent to levelling the Malvern Hills every five
years. These minerals are bulky and therefore costly to transport:
therefore they are quarried, mined and dug out of areas as close as
possible to where they are to be used. There is thus serious conflict
between the need for these materials and minerals and the objections
to the countryside being dug up, lorries churning up country lanes
and so on. Then there is the difficult problem of how much people
are prepared to pay for the kind of restoration that is always
possible in these sort of situations. How does one judge whether
one should allow a particular deposit to be used in a particular
circumstance? Besides these bulk minerals there are also scarcer
and more valuable minerals which may exist in various parts of this
country: nickel, lead, zinc, and so on. It is difficult to decide what
use we make of these resources when they are found in an area
which is particularly valuable from an environmental point of view
— a national park or an area of outstanding beauty. How do we

reconcile the conflicts in such a situation? Is it possible to make
use of cost-benefit analysis or some other technique in order to
decide what we should do in a particular situation? Some say we
should follow the road along which, in some respects, I think,
the United States has gone, of banning mineral extraction under
any circumstances in some areas. Here I think that we have to
make a judgement about our own national circumstances.
Extracting metals is an industry which, for one reason or another,
has been extinct for all practical purposes in this country, but is
now becoming of interest because the prices of metals have risen,
and because techniques have been evolved which can make deposits
economic which were formerly uneconomic. Should we mine these
deposits or leave them in the ground? My personal view is that it is
not possible to judge this in terms of absolute standards which
apply over large areas. What we must do is to take the particular
circumstances of each case, measure the economic circumstances
and the value of the potential employment to the area, and relate this
to a value judgement about the importance of that area in terms of
its natural beauty and so on. I do not think it is possible to escape
a value judgement about whether we should allow the mining
to proceed in whatever form is reasonably economic, and then to
decide in relation to that particular development what can be done
to protect the environment so far as is possible. It seems to me
that, almost by accident, we have evolved procedures in this
country through the planning laws which enable evidence to be
given on these issues, so enabling public opinion to be formed
about them, and finally enabling political judgement to be brought
to bear upon them. I think it is the right way to tackle these problems. I do not believe that it is possible to evolve standards which
have any meaning in relation to long periods of time, and I suggest
that we are right to go about them in our present pragmatic way.

What I have said refers in particular to opencast or 'strip'
mining, as the Americans call it. Excavations of this type are
usually shallow enough to allow the overburden to be put back

where the volume of mineral removed is not too large; and then a
high degree of restoration is possible. Examples in the United
Kingdom include both coal and iron-ore opencast mines. Where a
large volume of material is removed, as in quarrying, open-pit
mining for low-grade ores, or sand and gravel, or clay workings, the
problems of restoration are very much greater; indeed, it may then
be as well to accept the altered shape of the landscape and tackle
that by planting vegetation and landscaping.

## FACTORS INFLUENCING GOVERNMENT DECISIONS IN THE UNITED STATES  *G. MacDonald*

I would like to discuss public participation in the United States in
two kinds of decision-making process; one with specific respect to
standards, and the other with respect to general programmes,
projects or actions undertaken by government. In both cases
attempts have been made through our legislation to have these
processes operating as much as possible in 'goldfish bowl' conditions.
In the development of, say, air quality standards, there are prescribed
periods for the publication of standards, input after publication,
review of the input, and so forth. In the times set aside for discussion and in comments on the standards, consumer groups, environmental groups, as well as industrial groups, all participate, and
participate actively. We consider this to be one of the principal
experiments in government undertaken over two or three centuries.
We have tried to build into the decision-making process environmental consideration right from the start; that is, a decision on the
location of a highway or an airport, exemption of an excise tax on
automobiles, the granting of a licence or whatever will all be
exposed to the public for comment, whether through written
comment or through a series of public hearings. The procedures of
the National Environmental Policy Act require the government,
prior to making any substantial decision, to undertake a complete
environmental analysis and to make this analysis available to all

other government agencies with interests, expertise or jurisdiction
at the federal, state or local level. It is made available to any kind
of group of citizens or individual citizens that wish to examine or
comment on it. Then the responsible government agency must
collect this information, analyse it, carry through a cost-benefit
analysis, and present the information, with comments from the
public, to responsible officials. I think perhaps the best illustration
of how this works is the case of the Trans-Alaska pipeline. Here,
shortly after the enactment of the new law in January 1970, the
Department of the Interior filed a preliminary statement on the
environmental context of the pipeline. It was very preliminary and
very rough and, when the court looked at it, it was judged inadequate. The courts then returned the matter to the Department of
the Interior and told them to prepare a proper statement. Since
then I would guess approximately $20-25 million have been spent
by government and industry in a detailed assessment of the
environmental aspects of the pipeline; the environmental effects
(direct and indirect) of shipping down the West Coast; analysis by
National Security Council of the strategic implications of the
Alaskan oil resources; the economic consequence of development
or non-development, and so on. All this material will be made
available to the Secretary of the Interior and to the President prior
to making any decision. Every one of these papers will have been
available to the public and to other agencies for comment, and
their comments will be included and summarised in the final
report. Finally, a series of hearings have been held, both in
Washington and Alaska, on the various aspects, looking both at
benefits to Alaska and the rest of the country, as well as at the
possible dangers. We feel that this is really an experiment in trying
to build environmental considerations into the whole decision-
making process. It also requires the development of environmental
expertise within the government agency and a sensitivity within
to the comments of interested outside groups. How well the experiment will work we don't know, but this is a mechanism that

can better avail the public of an input into the day-to-day decision process within the federal domain.

I would like to go on to comment on Professor Cole's discussion of the conflict in use of waterways, rivers, estuaries and so forth; to describe the United States' experience of this, and to anticipate what is, in my mind, one of the changes in the way the United States will deal with such problems in the near future. In the past our waterways have been protected by legislation which gave the states responsibility for regulating and developing their use. A particular waterway would be designated for recreational use, amenity, industrial use, or whatever. Once the use or designation was given, the state would then prepare measures, such as control over discharge of effluent, to enable the designated use to be achieved. In practice their powers have proved inadequate in many cases. In recognition of this the administration this year introduced somewhat stronger legislation to give the federal government the responsibility of setting effluent standards, and developed a permit programme to ensure compliance with the standards. Congress, in this case the Senate, is taking a revolutionary step. It has gone further than this combination of use designation and effluent standards and combined a motion of effluent standards with two other motions. The first is that by 1983 all waters in the United States shall be safe to swim in and capable of supporting diversified aquatic life, which is an interesting goal: I'm not quite clear how we can get oyster beds into the Houston Ship Canal, but I suppose it can be done! The second goes beyond effluent standards *per se* and will require that by 1985 there shall be no discharge of any pollution into any waterway in the United States. The underlying notion here is that waters have no carrying capacity, and that you need to devise other schemes of disposing of waste, with a strong emphasis on recycling and on disposal of solid wastes on land. Our preliminary cost estimates of achieving the no-discharge requirement by industry are, needless to say, astronomical. However, I think that the mood of the country ensured the

passage of this legislation. There is a strong commitment to use
the two goals: the swimming goal and the discharge goal.

Let me now turn to Mr Lippitt's comments with regard to
mineral extraction, which has become increasingly difficult in the
United States as in the United Kingdom. We have had to try to
balance the various competing claims for the use of land or waters.
We have attempted, in an inadequate way, to carry out a cost-
benefit analysis, but in the end it has become a political decision.
Exploration of the Santa Barbara Channel oilfield was cancelled
after the government had leased thirty-five options for more than
$200 million to petroleum companies. We are in the process of
cancelling those leases, and long legal battles will undoubtedly
ensue. I recall flying over the channel with the head of the legal
department of Union Oil, and we saw oil pouring from a platform.
We looked at this vast display of oil on the waters and he said
'Ah, there is job security'. We are faced with a number of similar
decisions around the country where communities have designated
state areas of conservation and are asking federal government to
adopt policies consistent with local decisions. It is argued that,
where inland riverain areas are designated as conservation areas,
the federal lands to the seaward of them should be similarly
designated, and this indeed was the decisive argument in the case
of Santa Barbara. I think this is going to continue to be a
difficult issue.

We face very similar kinds of question elsewhere, and the public
are made very aware of them by the accelerated activities of strip
mining, mainly for coal. An increasing amount of coal supplies is
being derived from strip mines, and the machines used for this type
of mining are of gigantic proportions, eight or ten storeys high, and
they rumble along at a fantastic speed, gobbling up great areas of
the State of West Virginia, or wherever it may be, to the great concern of the local inhabitants, and increasingly of the federal
government. We have introduced legislation to regulate and require
the rehabilitation of land that has been so stripped. In the course of

the development of this legislation we did a comparative study of
strip and underground mining in terms of overall environmental
effects. One of the surprising outcomes of that study was that, if
you take into account all the features of underground mining, the
subsidence question, land drainage, human safety, it would seem to
us that, properly regulated, regulated strip mining is to be preferred
to unregulated underground mining. This is an important conclusion.
In our country there is a very strong pressure to ban strip mining outright, but, in my view, strip mining is preferable in that much of
the damage can in part be restored through backfilling and restoration. It is the policy of the present administration to develop
regulatory mechanisms whereby the environmental'damage
resulting from strip mining is kept at a national minimum rather
than to ban it.


## DISCUSSION

Discussion centred first on the 'trigger' for governmental action.
In what ways can governments forestall untoward consequences
of new technology and of more intensive exploitation of the
environment instead of reacting to calamaties that have already
occurred? How can the interval between the realisation of an
expected or actual untoward consequence and corrective action be
shortened without the risk of over-reaction or of remedies being
applied that produce fresh evils?

Mr Price said that whether we could organize ourselves so as to
avoid an unforseen mishap, a 'horror', depended to some extent on
the linkages between our research organisation and 'the point of
action'. In the case of atomic energy an organisation was created which
on the whole, showed itself to be well capable of looking forward.
This was even true of such a regrettable occurrence as the Windscale
reactor accident. One of his first tasks on joining Harwell had been
to work out what would happen if the Windscale reactor caught
fire. (Not that this was thought credible: the reason was simply a

desire to get an idea of the environmental hazard which might result, 'Just in case'.) As it happened, the chimney was already halfway up when the calculations began to make it clear that filters were needed in the outlet for the cooling air; and the chimney consequently took on a very curious shape, with the filters at the top — the only place left for them. But they proved their worth when the reactor did catch fire some years later. Subsequently the atomic energy industry built up an organisation specifically to look into all possible accidents. A fail-safe design philosophy was evolved; and the studies took into account the totality of the possible consequences, including ecological aspects. Mr Price felt sure that the existence of this design philosophy, coupled with the high quality effort that was available, had been instrumental in avoiding any really serious neclear accidents up to the present day. Nor had he any doubt that the atomic energy model was a good one, even though, in some respects, it was a little over-elaborate. In particular, any safety studies should be done in the context of the whole system (not only the engineering but also the vulnerable parts of the environment); and it must be possible to transmit the conclusions, when occasion demands, through fairly short communication links to the point of action.

Sir George Godber said that adverse factors in the environment could be detected relatively easily when they led to something akin to an outbreak of communicable disease. For instance, the occurrence of some fifty deaths in the area of Minimata Bay in Japan as a result of eating fish with a very high mercury content was associated with an illness of an unusual kind suggesting a local specific cause. There had been other examples of unusual illness resulting from specific contamination of food; for instance, accidental contamination of flour in transit as a result of leakage of a particular insecticide in the vehicle, with a resulting group of cases of illness with a most unusual symptomatology. The thalidomide disaster was one of the best-known examples of unsuspected adverse effects of a drug. Practically all the cases occurred within the space of about three and a half years. The lesions occurred, not in the patients, but in the babies born to women who had taken the drug early in pregnancy. The malformations which resulted were of a striking physical kind normally occuring with a very low incidence. When this was suddenly increased two or threefold, the unusual nature of the disability and the abrupt increase in incidence led fairly easily to the identification. Nevertheless, this point was not reached until some years after the first use of thalidomide for the control of vomiting in pregnancy.

The sort of problem with which we should be increasingly concerned in future was much less readily defined than this. Chronic degenerative diseases of a kind which occur without demonstrable specific cause, such as atherosclerosis and other than occupational cancers, had a base line of incidence which we had long been accustomed, perhaps erroneously, to regard as natural. Since they are fairly common conditions, we were likely to detect a causal relationship only when the site or nature of the lesion was unusual or a very large change in incidence occurred. The most obvious example of this was the relationship of cigarette smoking to lung cancer, chronic bronchitis and cardiovascular disease. Lung cancer had formerly been an unusual tumour. In the twenty years preceding 1950 the incidence had increased progressively and to such an extent that it was no longer possible to attribute the observed increase simply to better diagnosis. In the early 1950s, independently in North America and Britain, a clear statistical association between lung cancer and cigarette smoking was demonstrated. By the time it was fully accepted, a major epidemic of a malignant disease had developed. This has progressed further since, and we now know that we are dealing with a condition mainly, though not quite wholly, attributable to a particular causal factor but with an incubation period of 20-40 years (Fig. 5). When the causal relationship between smoking and lung cancer had been demonstrated, the parallel of chronic bronchitis was relatively easily identified and then the association with sudden deaths from myocardial infarction in middle-aged men at an earlier age than was usual from other causes. Thus the major and horrifying incident of an epidemic of malignant disease on this scale had led us to identify two other effects in producing chronic conditions which could also occur naturally without exposure to this particular causal agent.

If we expected to identify long-acting environmental causes of chronic degenerative conditions we needed some major or bizarre incident which pinpointed them for identification. Without the 'horror story' it might take much longer to relate cause to effect. For instance, in the 1960s an increase in deaths from asthma following the use of a particular inhalant under high pressure con- tinued for four or five years before the occurrence was noted and traced to its cause. It would be much more difficult to pinpoint relatively modest changes in incidence of familiar conditions as results of particular exposures. The relationship of soft water supplies to cardiovascular disease mortality was one current example of this.

Dr Holdgate said that we ought never to forget that the environ- ment is inclined suddenly to trip us up from time to time. Hence there were two inputs into the standard setting and regulatory process. Either somebody came up with a problem in an ordinary, on-going programme; or the environment confronted us with an unexpected 'horror situation' and somebody had to make provisional assessment in a hurry. For example, people died of 'Minamata disease' in Japan as a result of methyl mercury effluent contamin- ating estuarine fish. Such an event led to two things. First, government experts made an immediate assessment which by-passed national primary standards because, at that stage, nobody would know what the maximum real allowable intake of the pollutant was. Then, after a 'guesstimate' of uncertain quality, national derived working levels were set; in the Japanese case a code of practice saying 'do not eat fish from this area' and an emission control setting a limit on the amount of mercury released from the factory. An environmental quality standard was not set up at that point, for nobody was in a position to define the maximal allowable amount of mercury per cubic metre of water — and even if they could, it would not dispense with the need for the other two, more practical, standards. In Britain and other countries which did not suffer a Minamata episode, the course of logic would have been to say, 'The Japanese have had a nasty problem; we'd better study it and see if it occurs here'. In practice Professor Cole's department had surveyed mercury levels in fish around Britain so that the 'horror' in Japan created a research input in Britain which led to a scientific assessment which led in turn to decisions. The first was that it was inappropriate to set a national primary protection standard at that stage, and secondly that it was unnecessary to restrict the consumption of fish by a code of practice. It was necessary, nevertheless, to use the mechanism of the river authorities to review, and in some cases improve, the existing emission controls on the polluting industry; and this had, in fact, been done. There was one chlor-alkali works in this country which had reduced the mercury level in its effluent in the space of four months to around one per cent of what it was before.

There followed an exchange on the role of public opinion in influencing governmental decisions. Professor Beckerman referred to Dr MacDonald's description of the new pattern of consultation and opportunity for comment which was a major characteristic of recent legislation in the United States. A very similar mechanism to allow the involvement of the public in environmental decisions had operated in the United Kingdom over most of the postwar period. This involved the use of the public local inquiry, where there were objections to a planning decision, prior to a final decision by the minister. These local inquiries were generally conducted by inspectors from the Housing and Planning Inspectorate of the Department of the Environment. After the local hearing, the inspector reported to the minister, and at some later time the ministerial decision was given by letter. In some cases development involved a private bill, in which case there was opportunity for a

parliamentary debate. Further, major decisions, such as the site of
the Third London Airport, might now, following the Town and
Country Planning Act of 1968, be the subject of investigation by
Planning Inquiry Commissions, consisting of between three and
five members, which dealt with 'cases that raise wide or novel
issues of more than local significance'. One aspect of all such inquiries was the way in which public opinion should be tested.
While the local public inquiry allows the parading of such elements
of public opinion, the decision-making processes of government on
environmental matters that do not involve the planning law do not
go on in such a public forum. Who speaks for the consumer on
such occasions? Mr Chilver suggested that the answer to Professor
Beckerman's question lay in central and local democracy. For
example, in present circumstances central government would require strong reasons for intensifying control of pollution in ways
that accelerated price and wage inflation or added to unemployment. Decisions about abatement of pollution rested to some extent
with local government; and the fact that standards and practices
were not uniform throughout the country illustrated local democracy at work. Admittedly, interest in local democracy was at
present at a low ebb, because units of local government were often
too small and their boundaries obsolete, especially boundaries
separating town from the country areas round them. One consequence had been unduly frequent intervention by central government, and many people had come to think that all important
decisions were taken centrally. The legislation on local government
organisation currently before parliament could be expected to
reverse these trends. He would add that democracy did not of
course, operate only at election times. He had pointed out earlier
that protecting the environment competed for resources with other
social objectives. A proposal to build a reservoir rather than meet a
need for water in some more expensive way might be strongly
opposed by a minority on grounds of amenity, while the majority
showed no interest in the matter, which might perhaps be taken as

implying that they favoured other uses for the expenditure at issue. In such a case the decision would not necessarily go against the minority. Nor should it: the strength with which opinions are held is a valid democratic factor.

# 5: International Processes

Mr Arculus here examines the roles of international co-operation
in protecting the environment, and in particular distinguishes
between the fields in which mandatory international standards for
products or practices are appropriate and those where international
discussions are better confined to consultation and the exchange
of information with a view to individual national action; and discusses the organisation of these activities. Mr Serwer, speaking as a
member of the secretariat of the United Nations Conference on
the Human Environment, explains the secretariat's thinking about
the scope for international standards and the means of formulating
them. M. Carpentier describes the fields of activity in environmental
protection which the Commission of the European Economic Community has recently proposed for itself and is discussing with
member and candidate-member governments of the Community.
These include not only the control of pollution, but activities
designed to influence the distribution of population and industry
and the use of land in socially desirable directions. Mr Langley
gives an industrialist's opinion on the role that international organ-
izations most usefully play in controlling pollution, and suggests
things that should be avoided.

In the discussion that followed there was no disagreement that
international standards, ranging from global ones to bilateral ones,
are indispensable where pollution crosses national frontiers, and

where polluting products are important articles of international trade. Doubt was expressed about the wisdom of formal international agreements outside these two fields, though it was recognised that national control of pollution was no exception to the growing tendency of one country's economic actions to affect another's. Room was seen for improvement in the international mechanics for consultation and for pooling the results of research.

## INTERNATIONAL DECISION-MAKING *W. Beckerman*

Many alleged economic problems arising out of the economics of pollution abatement are often more apparent than real. For example, it is often argued that a country that introduces pollution controls (in any form) will be worse off if others do not follow suit, insofar as it will reduce the competitiveness of that country.[1] As a prediction of what will follow from pollution restrictions this may be quite valid, but as an economic argument against such action it is not. No doubt the same arguments have been used throughout the last two centuries or more in opposition to the abolition of slavery, or child labour, or the introduction of safety regulations in factories, or for paying workmen a living wage. It would always add to costs and, if others did not follow suit, it would reduce competitiveness. But, from the national or social point of view, this cannot be any justification for *not* covering social costs.

In general there is no justification for selling goods to foreigners at a price that does not cover all our social costs (at the margin). To do this means reducing real income, not raising it. Other countries obtain the benefit of consuming our goods at prices that do not recoup us for all our (marginal) social costs of producing them, including our pollution costs. The optimum trade policy for a country is to maximise profits on its exports, not to sell some of them at a loss, which is what happens if the price of exports does not cover the (marginal) social cost of pollution incurred in the production of the goods. Hence, if polluters are charged the social costs of pollution and if, as they should, they add these to their total costs, which are then reflected in their prices, foreigners have to pay for our full social (marginal) costs of production, including the social costs of the pollution, in the same way as they are expected to pay for the full costs of the labour and materials used in their production.

Of course, at the corresponding level of export prices, we might sell fewer goods and if we were in equilibrium to begin with this could lead to an unacceptable balance of payments deficit. But this is no more reason for not charging the pollution costs than it would be for not charging the full costs of the labour or materials embodied in any exports. If we do not achieve our foreign balance target, this will generally be a matter of the level of demand in the economy and, more probably, the exchange rate (given overseas conditions etc). Thus, if optimal policies are adopted in each country to deal with pollution, the pattern of international trade will be optimal as well (other things being equal, of course). Indeed, it is when exports do *not* reflect pollution costs, together with all other costs, that the pattern of international trade is sub-optimal and to the detriment of the polluting country. If the foreign balance had been in equilibrium before the social costs of pollution were reflected in export prices, then the level of demand or the exchange rate must have been wrong! For it could not have been the level of demand or the exchange rate that achieved the desired balance when the export prices are *correct* — ie reflect full domestic costs in each line of production and, therefore, reflect accurately that country's comparative advantage.

*Uniform international standards*

If other countries do not follow suit when a given country introduces the anti-pollution measures appropriate to that particular country, then they are not acting in *their* interests. For they are selling goods to others, including us, at prices which do not fully compensate for their costs. (But we do not necessarily gain from this. Total world output is reduced below optimum output, and it is not certain that we will not share in some of this loss). Furthermore, there is no reason to expect all countries to adopt the same pollution standards even if they were to follow optimum policies. The point at which the marginal social costs of abatement equal the social costs of pollution may vary from country to country, and hence the appropriate charge for pollution or the appropriate degree of abatement will vary from country to country. World optimisation requires that goods are produced in different countries according to the respective national patterns of comparative advantage. Hence, if the production of, say, steel can be carried out in some country where its social costs of pollution (at the optimum) are negligible, it is quite right that world steel production should tend to be concentrated there rather than in a country where the pollution may be very heavy and where a high charge would have to be imposed. It is thus desirable that a high charge be imposed in the latter country but not in the former. If both were obliged to apply the same charge, there is no incentive to shift steel production to the countries which, by virtue of being low polluters, have a comparative advantage in steel output. To take the opposite view is like saying that no country shall obtain an 'unfair' advantage from its fortunate position with respect to the production of wine or wheat just because its costs of producing these goods are lower than elsewhere and that, since other countries could only produce wine or wheat at a high social cost, France and the USA should raise the prices of their wine and wheat respectively in order not to have an 'unfair' advantage.

However, there is one genuine problem in connection with the international aspects of pollution. This is the case of transnational pollution: ie the case where several countries share the same area (such as the North Sea); or the same river basin (eg the USA and Canada, or the countries bordering the Rhine); or influence each other's atmosphere (eg Scandinavian fears that their atmosphere is being poisoned by $SO_2$ from the rest of Europe). This is a com-

pletely different matter from the effect on international trade. In
such cases, some or all of the pollution is not merely external to
the firm or the industry, but is external to the country, so that
there is no more incentive for the country responsible for the
pollution to allow for the external pollution costs than in the case
of the factory owner whose smoky chimney spoils somebody
else's laundry. In the same way that national optimum is not
achieved in the presence of uncorrected externalities, so world
optimum is not achieved if transnational externalities are not
corrected. In such cases there is a clear need for international
agreement. There are obvious difficulties, but in cases where the
interaction is uni-directional — eg if British $SO_2$ affects Sweden but
not the other way round — it is highly likely that the extra costs
to British producers of meeting the Swedish social costs of British
air pollution would be negligible by comparison with the pollution
costs incurred in Britain; though this is not necessarily always the
case — eg with high chimney policies. Cases where the burden on
other countries is considerable are likely to be cases — such as a
shared river basin — where the effect is in both directions, in that
each can and does pollute the other.

In such cases the theory is interesting, in that it resembles a
duopoly situation or game theory situation. If country X increases
its pollution, does country Y pollute even less to offset it, or
pollute even more because there is now less point in virtuous
abstinence? In such cases it is clear that mutual negotiation is
required, but the condition of reciprocal effect should mean that
agreement should not be impossible to reach. (There is a long
history of Canadian-USA co-operation over pollution of shared
rivers).[2]

One of the side issues that emerges from the international trade
effect of anti-pollution policies is the so-called 'danger' that some
polluting activities will be transferred to less developed countries.
If this is because the social costs of pollution abatement (at the
optimum) in the developed countries have become much higher

than in some developing countries (which may reflect either higher abatement costs or higher relative evaluation of the social costs of pollution in a country where other needs are less pressing etc) then it is desirable that production of the product concerned should shift to the developing country. The principle that world optimisation requires that production should be concentrated according to the world pattern of comparative advantage applies here, and its application is to the advantage even of the developing country as long as the local pollution costs are included in the prices charged by the developing country (unless they are too small to justify the administrative effort and other costs of implementation). In the past, changes in the world pattern of comparative advantage have tended to lead to a redistribution of, say, world textile production towards certain developing countries. In the same way a change in the comparative advantage of producing goods that pollute might enable developing countries where the optimum level of pollution charges would be low (because of either different environmental conditions or different priorities), to take advantage of this shift in comparative costs patterns and to produce and export goods that, hitherto, would be beyond their competitive power.

### *International decision-making* R. Arculus

A start has been made on rationalising international work in the many organisations concerned. It is easy enough to suggest a rational division, but hard to enforce it. The international secretariats are anxious to share in the work; the membership of organisations varies; the industrialised nations are in the minority in the larger global organisations, and some governments find it difficult to ensure that experts and non-governmental representatives in particular, take a line consistent with central policy. Basically we hope that economic work will be concentrated in OECD; ECE can be used for certain standards-setting work on the lines of that which has been done in Geneva in the past; sectoral organisations should be used where appropriate, eg ICAO, IMCO, WMO; regional work may be the most effective and appropriate in some cases, eg marine pollution in the North Sea area, the Mediterranean, the Adriatic. ISO should continue with its work. In the first instance future UK policy will need to be looked at in the EEC framework; this group contains our environmental neighbours and our main industrial customers and competitors.

Where national action may set up non-tariff barriers, the usual international machinery is available. The early warning system in OECD is designed to prevent such problems arising in the limited field of bioactive substances, although the scheme may be extended later.

UK doctrine on international emission and product standards has been set out in a paper for the OECD Environmental Committee, and has been made available to the principal governments concerned as well as to the secretary-general of the UN Conference on the Human Environment (Stockholm 1972). Most industrialised countries are acutely aware of the need to avoid trade disadvantages flowing from the setting of environmental standards. The US have made particular efforts to carry the Japanese Government with them, so that the gap between American and Japanese manufacturing costs is not widened by the application of lower standards in Japan. The Germans, Dutch and others are very conscious of the need to justify to their industry the need for accepting higher standards by pointing to approximately equal burdens which will be imposed on their industrial competitors. The French are particularly anxious not to accept unnecessary burdens on their industry. The Swedes appear to be one of the most radical in urging severe controls and to contemplate subsidies and other incentives, but may encounter resistance from some of their industries. There are increasing international industrial contacts in this field.

Work on the cost of pollution controls, and analysis of the 'principle' that the polluter should pay, has begun in OECD, which is also to tackle the question of transnational frontier pollution problems, which are particularly important to the countries of

continental Europe. A special study has also been started of this
problem in the pulp and paper industry where pollution control
costs are particularly high. The EEC and the US are jointly to
study the chemical industry in this regard.


## INTERNATIONAL DECISION-MAKING   *D. P. Serwer*

As the representative of the secretary-general of the United Nations
Conference on the Human Environment, I would like to discuss
briefly the present state of the preparations for action at Stockholm
on what we are calling here 'the formulation and implementation
of environmental standards'. The secretariat is fortunate in having
had extensive advice from the 27-nation Preparatory Committee in
the preparation of the proposal on pollution control. The Preparatory
Committee has provided, among other things, a set of agreed terms and
definitions. On the basis of this guidance, we at the United Nations
Institute for Training and Research and in the Conference Secretariat
have developed an over-all approach to what we call 'International
Co-operation for Pollution Control' which follows this introduction.

In its bare outlines, this looks like an extreme form of what we
might call the 'rational approach', which includes weighing costs
and benefits and the control of sources of pollution in such a way
that explicit primary protection standards based on this weighing
are not exceeded. In putting some flesh on this skeleton, however,
we included a number of elements of what might be called the
'pragmatic approach'; that is, one that concentrates on controlling
sources of pollution. For instance, it is emphasised that it should
be axiomatic that, whether a primary protection standard has been
developed or not, the levels of a pollutant in the environment
should be kept as low as is readily achievable, economic and social
factors being taken into account. We have also included guidance as
to when and why sources should be controlled, even in the absence
of a primary protection standard: 'When the benefits of avoiding
specified risks are thought to outweigh the cost'. Even in the

'rational' skeleton, we do not make the stipulation that net benefits should be maximised, but rather that the benefits of limiting a pollutant to a given level should exceed the costs. Maximization is asking a great deal too much, given the uncertainties in even a very detailed cost-benefit analysis on problems of this type. Moreover, we are not suggesting that cost-benefit analyses necessarily be done, but rather that the justification for taking action to control sources should be based on judgement as to what the costs and benefits are, supported by as much data as can be readily obtained or as it is worthwhile to obtain. The decision to do a cost-benefit analysis should itself be subjected to some cost-benefit thinking; very often one may conclude that the analysis is not worthwhile. Even incomplete data may, however, be useful. As others here have pointed out, the benefits of avoiding the risks posed by a pollutant are often unknown. But the costs of avoiding risks – that is, the costs of controlling polluters – are often available, at least in part. Estimates of such costs at least give an idea of how big the benefits have to be in order to justify action.

It is our present thinking that, for a limited number of pollutants of international significance, quantitative assessments should be performed by intergovernmental expert bodies of the United Nations. The active participation of other concerned international organisations would be encouraged, but the United Nations would be responsible for such comprehensive assessments, since it is not limited to considering only certain types of risks, media or sources, as are virtually all the specialised agencies. Such assessments would be done by intergovernmental bodies in order that sufficient resources be made available and in order that the assessments done receive widespread acceptance. One might object that politics would interfere, but past experience indicates clearly that extraneous political considerations are quickly left behind, if the effort is properly organised and conducted on the appropriate technical level. The benefits to governments of pooling their resources to perform the difficult and complex assessments required are apparent.

In deciding where to go beyond assessments of this type, the phrase 'pollution problems of international significance' is of great importance. If all pollution problems were of international significance, we would clearly be in trouble, since the capacity to deal with pollution control on the international level is extremely limited. In 'International Co-operation for Pollution Control', we have tried to indicate what types of pollution problems should be considered of international significance: those whose effects are felt beyond the national jurisdictions in which the pollutants are released to the environment (a formulation that is more general than the simpler 'pollutants that are distributed beyond the national jurisdictions in which they are released to the environment' since it includes a case like fish stocks, exploited by more than one state, but affected by pollutants only within the national jurisdiction in which these are released into the environment); those whose control affects international trade, whether because of the added costs to the producer of pollution control measures or because of the imposition in different countries of varying standards for goods or for their transport or use; and those that occur in many states. The number of problems that may fall in these categories, in particular the last, is very great, but we have suggested that there should be an intergovernmental body that would, among other things, screen problems that are of possible international significance and refer these to appropriate forums, whether inside or outside the United Nations systems, for action. It is of interest to note that, despite considerable effort, we have failed to come up with a formula that combines characteristics of pollutants like persistence, toxicity and mobility, and thereby tells what pollutants are of international significance. Such formulae could well be helpful in indicating probable candidates for 'international significance', but ultimately the decision as to what is of international significance depends not on the characteristics of the pollutant itself but on the circumstances in which the pollutant finds itself.

The usefulness of stating why pollutants are of international significance does not end with the guidance this gives in limiting the number of problems that are dealt with at the international level. It is also helpful in indicating possible solutions to these problems. Thus, for instance, pollutants that are of international significance because of their international distribution may require international co-operation, not only in developing limits for the levels of the pollutants in various media, but also in controlling sources. Otherwise, the limits may not be met or one state may bear an inequitable burden in meeting them. On the other hand, for pollution problems of international significance because the costs of control may put one state at a competitive disadvantage in international trade, there would appear to be no justification for imposing the same source controls. At most, what appears to be needed is that two competitive states agree to allow no more than a given level of pollution. Imposing the same source controls would vitiate advantages that a state may derive from having relatively low levels of a pollutant in the environment, whether due to meteorological or hydrological conditions, or to relative underdevelopment. I hasten to add that the degree to which these solutions need to be formulated as binding obligations also varies with the reasons for considering problems to be of international significance. Where commonly occuring local problems are concerned, there would appear to be a need for international standards, like those WHO has developed for drinking-water, that governments can utilise in formulating national legislation, but intergovernmental agreements appear both unlikely and unnecessary On the other hand, where international trade in products that may contain potential pollutants is concerned, states may find that some degree of intergovernmental agreement is needed, as is the case already for the Codex Alimentarius standards for food traded internationally. Without going into any more detail on this complex subject of the implementation of international environmental standards, I would emphasise that binding force is no warrant of compliance in international affairs. Standards, in our view, are a measure of what is acceptable or unacceptable, irrespective of binding force, and the effectiveness of international standards depends only in part on binding force.

As is apparent from some of the examples I have used, a good deal of work is already under way on the formulation of environmental standards by international organisations. It is not surprising that there are co-ordination problems among these organisations. Two types of co-ordination problems should be distinguished: one is the traditional problem of conflicting or overlapping jurisdictions; the other is the problem of assuring that needed environmental standards are developed and that those developed are consistent with each other. In my opinion, the first type of co-ordination problem is alleged far more often than it is proven. When overlap and conflict do occur, governments must share the blame with international organisations. It is, after all, governments that approve conflicting or overlapping programmes of the international organisations of which they are members, and it is governments that have constructed a United Nations system with a minimum of central authority. The second type of co-ordination problem is both intellectually more interesting and organizationally more important. Competence to deal with almost any pollution problem exists in the United Nations system: if a pollutant affects man, there is WHO; if it affects fish, there is FAO; if it is found in rivers, there is the Resources and Transport Division of the United Nations; if it is released from industry, there is UNIDO; if its control affects international trade, there are UNCTAD and GATT. The problem is that any single pollutant can do all of these things. As a result, we have a problem of mobilising existing competence to do what needs to be done in a consistent way. This mobilisation can, we think, be promoted by a small but vigorous apparatus, located in the United Nations itself, that follows particular pollutants from their various sources through the media in which they are transported to the organisms and resources that they ultimately

affect. Such an apparatus would weave a thread through the United
Nations system and strengthen the existing cloth by filling gaps and
tying together scattered activities.


## THE STANDARDS POLICY OF THE EEC IN RELATION TO
## UK ENTRY  *M. Carpentier*

To begin with, I shall discuss briefly the present activities of the
three Communities, namely the ECSC, EURATOM and EEC,
relating to the protection of environment. Then I shall comment on
a recent communication of the Commission on the whole field of
environmental problems, and I shall conclude by saying a few words
on the effects of both the existing and the proposed EEC policies
on the UK standards policy, insofar as such a standards policy
exists.

For a long time now each of the three Communities – ECSC,
EURATOM and EEC – has been engaged in certain activities relating to the protection of the environment within its own respective province.


*ECSC Activities*

The activities stemming from the ECSC Treaty have proceeded
in accordance with Article 55 of this treaty which states that the
ECSC must promote technical and economic research on safety in
the industries within its terms of reference, and that it shall arrange
to this end any relevant contacts between existing research bodies.

Since 1956 several research programmes and also individual
projects have been furthered with ECSC backing, ie have been
granted funds levied by the high authority in the mining and steel
industries. These programmes are devoted wholly or in part either
to a technical campaign aimed at protecting workers against
dangerous emissions of dust (mining and steelmaking) and gas
(steelmaking), or to research into, and organisation of, medical
action of a prophylactic or therapeutic nature.

The bulk of the research into anti-pollution techniques was directed towards the following:

1    determining the nature and extent of atmospheric pollution both inside and outside factories;

2    developing new processes or perfecting plant and products designed to forestall or combat atmospheric pollution in steelworks and mines;

3    examining the possibility of improving and standardising measuring techniques, methods and equipment;

4    carrying out research with the object of extending knowledge.

Apart from these latter aims, almost all of the research had practical objectives. Cases in point are the researching, development and finally the industrial implementation of various processes for the elimination of brown fumes and the removal of dust during the discharge and extinguishing of coke.

In the medical sphere, studies on the effects of pollutants on communities of workers have proved indispensable in (a) ensuring effective early medical prevention, and (b) tracing the correlation between pollution, the nature and frequency of respiratory disorders, and consequently the connection between the technical campaign, the drop in mortality figures and the improvement in working conditions in the coal and steel industries.

Funds provided by the levy upon iron and steelmaking (82 per cent) and mining (18 per cent), and the collaboration organised between engineers doctors, economists and statisticians, together with the co-operation of the national administrations, enabled this work to be performed at a Community level.

For the technical research in the social sector funds of 14,091,071 u.a. (=$) were allotted and for medical research for the first three programmes 15,000,000 u.a.

*EURATOM Activities*

The EURATOM Treaty contains a whole section dealing with

the protection of both population and workers against the health hazards resulting from ionizing radiation.

Basic standards — a term taken to mean maximum permissible doses, maximum permissible values for the contamination of the air and water, and the basic principles underlying the medical surveillance of workers — are laid down by the Council in accordance with proposals put forward by the Commission after consultations with a scientific working party and the Economic and Social Committee (Articles 30 and 31). These basic standards must then be incorporated in the laws, regulations and administrative provisions of the member states, the Commission making every recommendation with a view to ensuring the standardisation of these provisions (Article 33).

This creation of basic standards is accompanied by a series of regulations designed to ensure that each state will:

1    strengthen health protection measures in the case of particularly dangerous experiments, especially where the effects of these experiments are likely to affect the territory of the other member states (the official approval of the Commission is required in this latter instance);

2    provide the installations necessary for the continuous monitoring of the level of radioactivity in the atmosphere, the water and the soil and for ensuring that the basic standards are respected. The Commission has the right to enter these monitoring stations, check their operation and efficiency and receive information on these monitoring operations (Articles 35 and 36),

3    pass on general data concerning any planned release of radioactive waste (Article 37) for the attention of the Commission, who are assisted by a group of experts.

In addition, the Commission has the right to address to the member states any recommendations concerning the level of radioactivity in the atmosphere, water and soil and in an emergency to issue directives which the member states are bound to to observe on pain of proceedings by the Court of Justice.

By 1 June 1970 a total of sixty-seven plans for the discharge of radioactive waste had been submitted to the Commission under Article 37 of the EURATOM Treaty. In each instance a working party from the Six and the Commission examine every standard which can facilitate determination of whether implementation of the projects is likely to give rise to radioactive contamination of the water, soil or atmosphere of another member state. It then sends the member state concerned a detailed report within six months on the probability of such hazards and also where appropriate, recommendations on their restriction.

The first basic standards were drawn up in February 1959. Since then the directives laying down the basic standards have been amplified and amended on two occasions and a new version is currently being prepared. By 1 June 1970 the member states had submitted almost fifty draft regulations for examination and approval in application of these directives.

A certain number of secondary standards based on the original standards have been drawn up, notably dealing with maximum permissible concentrations of radionuclides in the atmosphere and water. The organisation of means for controlling and monitoring the levels of pollution of the air, water, soil and foodstuffs requires the full co-ordination, and in certain cases, the standardisation of measuring radioactivity in the various environments where this is of interest from a health point of view. A co-ordinated network of established and pilot-stations for measuring ambient radioactivity is currently in existence in the six member states. They regularly send details of their readings to the Community so that they can be studied, comparative analyses performed and mean values for the Community established.

This action is rounded off by a programme of research being conducted in three separate fields: co-ordination, promotion and encouragement of research.

*EEC Activities*
*Removal of technical barriers to trade and of distortion of conditions of competition*

The achievement of the aims of the Treaty of Rome presupposes action aimed at the removal of the economic barriers between the member states and the establishing of a system to prevent the distortion of conditions of competition within the Common Market.

It is mainly through basing its policies on similar considerations of competition and economic policy that the EEC has become involved in the field of pollution, with regard to the effects, which the discrepancies between the laws, regulations and administrative provisions taken by the member states with a view to reducing or eliminating pollutants, can have on trade competition.

As regards the products likely in themselves or in their use to have noxious effects on mankind or his environment, certain measures taken by the national authorities in this connection may be such that either their effects are equivalent to quantitative restrictions as defined in Articles 30 et seq, since they provide for the discriminatory treatment of national and imported products, or they are tantamount to technical barriers to trade, not because of the discriminatory treatment of the products according to their origin, but simply because of their disparity. These disparities stem from the application of Articles 30 et seq, in the first instance, and in the second from Article 100, in conjunction with the general programme adopted by the Council on 28 May 1969 for the elimination of the technical barriers to inter-Community trade in industrial products and foodstuffs. This programme specifies certain applications of Article 100 of the Treaty with a view to harmonising the measures taken by national authorities concerning these products. These measures are sometimes very dated and not generally concerned with the problems raised by the environment, which are more recent and have emerged gradually as industrial development has progressed.

During the course of this harmonisation it is, however, logical and necessary to take into consideration the aims pursued by the member states, as they form the basis for the various bodies of legislation to be dovetailed.

These aims may well vary from one member state to another, so that it is necessary to examine to what extent they are of value and geared to present-day requirements. It is against this background that the Commission has sometimes directed its attention at certain pollution problems, even if they were not directly covered by the legislation to be harmonised.

This is especially the case where pollutants, such as dangerous compounds (pesticides, solvents), gas pipelines (air pollution), oil pipelines (water pollution) and fertilizers, are concerned.

Moreover, recent legislation directly related to the protection of the environment must not be excluded. When such laws are directed towards products included in the general programme (eg motor vehicles, detergents), as was recently the case, the Commission was informed of their existence while they were still at the draft stage. Since these laws had a bearing on trade between member states, the Commission prepared a draft directive after requesting the member state(s) concerned to postpone the adoption of their draft.

This draft directive must be adopted by the Council in accordance with the procedure laid down in Article 100 within a very short period of time, in line with the undertaking given by the representatives of the member states at the meeting of the Council held on 28 May 1969.

Directives relating to the following have already been adopted to date:

permissible noise level and motor vehicle exhaust systems;

pollution of the atmosphere by automotive petrol engines;

and several proposals for directives dealing with toxic emissions or pollutants are currently under examination by the Council or are being prepared by the departments of the Commission with a view to their being adopted fairly soon, ie:

dangerous substances (solvents, pesticides, etc);

household products;
gas pipelines (atmospheric pollution);
oil pipelines (water pollution);
air pollution due to automotive diesel engines;
fertilizers;
the composition of the petrol for use in motor vehicles
(mainly the lead content);
the biodegradability of detergents;
radio-electrical interference.

From the point of view of damage to human health and the
natural environment caused by production processes, the measures
taken at national level can likewise have a direct bearing on the
functioning of the Common Market as a result of their disparity.
The conditions of competition can be distorted, as a result of an
unequal apportionment of the cost involved in the fight against
pollution, or the setting of standards at different levels for similar
geographical and ecological conditions, or by the abuse of favourable geographical conditions.

The efforts were initially concentrated on regulations aimed at
combating pollution of water. The Commission has had comparative
studies carried out of the legislation in this field in the member
states and has tried to assess the economic repercussions of its
application. Moreover, the Community has likewise become
involved with pollution through its common policies, and particularly through its agricultural policy.

Certain measures taken or proposed under the common policies
concern directly or indirectly the conservation or improvement of
the environment. Such measures relate especially to agricultural
policy. Three basic problems have been taken into consideration:
that concerning the quality of foodstuffs; another relating to
environmental pollution due to agriculture and, finally, that of the
management and conservation of the natural environment.

Since 1963 several regulations dealing with colorants, preservatives
and anti-oxidants in foodstuffs and additives in animal foodstuffs

have been adopted by the Council.

Since 1968, proposed regulations dealing with residual pesticides in fruit and vegetables, as well as undesirable constituents of animal foodstuffs, have been submitted by the Commission to the Council, where they are currently under discussion. Other drafts — concerning in particular residual pesticides in cereals, regulations governing the use of substances with an oestrogenic or thurostatic action, and also the approval and distribution of phytopharmaceutical products — are being studied by working parties of the Commission with a view to their submission to the Council. It should be noted that the Commission shortly intends to submit a draft directive to the Council which includes a ban on the use of certain persistent pesticides.

These texts were prepared as part of the work on the integration of legislation, with a view not only to removing technical barriers to trade and raising productivity, but also to improving the quality of the agricultural product marketed in the Community.

To this end fundamental importance is attached to consumer health protection. All of the standards adopted or proposed on the subject of additives, undesirable substances and residual pesticides have been set in accordance with the acceptable daily doses worked out by the FAO and WHO working parties and also the respective diets characterising the different countries of the Community. In addition, all of these proposals submitted to the Council are passed for perusal to the consumers' associations grouped together within the Community. It has been noted that the tolerances proposed by the Commission on the subject of residual pesticides are often lower than those currently authorised in North America.

The part played by agriculture in the pollution of the environment appears to be restricted mainly to the use of certain persistent insecticides of the chlorinated organic type and certain herbicides in the phenoxyacetic acid group. Currently several countries are taking, or plan to take, controlling measures aimed at banning or restricting the use of these products.

The departments of the Commission are examining the possibility of replacing persistent pesticides by rapidly degradable pesticides as part of their work of harmonising the approval and marketing of phytopharmaceutical products.

Additionally, the Commission has already expressed the opinion that it would be advisable to promote research aimed at taking advantage of the biological and integrated campaigns, and farming methods helping to cut down on the use of chemical pesticides. The advisability of drawing up, at Community level, an accelerated research programme devoted to these questions must be studied as quickly as possible.

The proposals dealing with agricultural reform recently submitted by the Commission can help to conserve the environment and to create recreation areas. Directive B, on incentives for leaving the land and the reallocation of farmland used for the purpose of improving the structure of agricultural holdings, lays down a new rule, namely, that grants for leaving the land are conditional upon the land thus made available being reallocated, not only for enlarging the size of other holdings but also for non-agricultural purposes, such as afforestation, recreational and leisure areas, national parks, etc. These aids are partly financed from the EAGGF.

The maintenance of a minimum farming population, notably in mountainous regions, warrants special support measures, unrelated to usual standards of productivity, which most mountain farms cannot meet because of natural conditions. The new forms of support which can be applied in mountainous regions must be adapted to the circumstances in which the farmers find themselves, especially with regard to age. Certain measures have already been proposed as part of agricultural reform:

1    Incentive payments to ageing farmers on cessation of agricultural activity, the holdings of whom could enable younger men (who have been leaving in large numbers up to the present) to remain in agriculture by extending their holdings. It should be noted that the recipients of these

bonuses will remain *in situ* and continue to live in their traditional dwellings as hitherto.

2    Investment aids to young men who modernise their
holdings. This aid facilitates reorientation output towards
quality products which are typical of the region.

3    Aid towards professional retraining (promoting the
gaining of qualifications necessary to the practice of pro-
fessions connected with the tourist industry).

Another measure of a completely new nature is in preparation,
namely, outright grants in aid, irrespective of output, to be paid to
farmers who are unable to modernise and who have not reached the
age entitling them to an early-retirement bonus.

This list of activities shows that the Communities are not
entirely lacking either in a certain experience or in all powers to act
to protect and improve the environment. The analysis makes it clear,
however, that the measures available to the European Community,
although not inconsiderable, are limited to particular sectors and
problems, and furthermore differ in nature and scope as between
treaties.

That is why, in a communication dated July 1971, the Commission set out for the first time what, in its opinion, the objectives
and means of the European Community should be in the field of
environment protection. This communication has been transmitted
to the appropriate authorities, and to the economic and professional circles in the member states and the candidate countries,
with a view to obtaining any useful comments and suggestions. It
has also been forwarded for information to the European Parliament,
the Council of Ministers and the Economic and Social Committee.

On the basis of information obtained — and, I can say, I have
received some here — the Commission will later draft concrete proposals for the Council concerning fulfilment of the aims set out in
the communication.

The drafting of this communication and of future proposals is
supervised by a working group of Commissioners under Mr Spinelli,

and carried out by my department in co-operation with a working group of specialised departments, of which I am chairman.

This environmental programme has of necessity a dominantly political character. It cannot be limited to the definition and harmonisation of technical questions and standards; but deals primarily with the degree of priority to be set between the justified interests of individuals or single groups and the competing claims of the population as a whole. We think that, in an increasingly populous, urbanised and industrialised society, the environment can no longer be viewed just as an external medium to whose noxious influences we have to submit, but as a datum indissoluble from the organisation and promotion of the progress of mankind.

The environmental programme set out by the Commission is based on the following principles:

1    Free exchange of products and free competition within the Community could be prevented by unco-ordinated actions of the member states. According to the rules of the Common Market, all its participants should be subject to the same conditions and restrictions, or at least to the same harmonised regulations which take into account special local or regional circumstances.

2    In order to utilise public funds efficiently and to prevent divergent national developments, all costly research should be co-ordinated at Community level, and certain research projects should be carried out jointly. The existing capacities of the Joint Research Centre could be helpful.

3    The execution of the jointly decided policy must be by common bodies, and control could be similarly organised.

4    The possibilities offered by a harmonised fiscal policy within the Community should be used as an instrument for reducing pollution.

5    The member countries, regions, cities and towns should be given large competences in the field of environment protection and its execution.

6    A common environmental policy cannot be limited to fighting against pollution and annoyances. Special efforts will have to be made to arrive at a more equilibrated regional qualitative distribution of economic activities within the member countries by using all the possibilities at the Community's disposal. To solve this problem, the requirements of the Community's industrial policy, agricultural policy and regional policy must be aligned.

7    Throughout the world, environmental questions are gaining increasing political priority. That is why the Community's services have closely collaborated for some time with international organisations, such as OECD, ECE, Council of Europe, NATO, GATT and the United Nations, and they refrain from carrying out studies covering the same ground as those conducted by these bodies.

In the Commission's opinion a general action programme of the Community in the field of environment protection should include the following points:

1    Establishment of environmental regulations at European Community level aiming at the reduction or elimination of risks entailed by pollutions or disutilities on human health and well-being.

2    Organisation of a community network of observation stations for water, air and soil pollution — based on existing national installations — and the foundation of a common observation data processing centre allowing for complete and comparable information on pollution levels and an effective control of common regulations in the Community.

3    Definition of a co-ordinated research programme with the possible financial participation of the Community aiming at:

   — improving the knowledge on pollution phenomena, necessary for establishing the above-mentioned community regulations;

- improving methods and techniques of measurement
- developing new non-polluting or less polluting industrial products and processes.

4    Co-operation of the member states in order to enforce the observation of the anti-pollution laws by individuals and to harmonise measures against infractions of these laws.

5    Possible financial aid on easy terms for special efforts on regional and sectorial level in fighting against pollutants.

6    Preservation and management of natural resources of the Community in the framework of agriculture and regional policy.

7    Promotion of land-use control in certain regions of general interest to the Community (eg the Rhine river basin and the coastal regions), and financial participation in the creation and maintenance of control and development agencies for these regions.

8    Participation of the Community as such in work done by international organisations aiming at:

- the conservation of world natural resources,
- avoiding barriers of international trade and thus pre-serving the Community's interests.

9    Study of the advantages resulting from the creation of a European Institute for the Environment, taking into account the different efforts made in this direction in the member states. This institute could co-ordinate at Community level studies and research in the field of environmental protection.

The complexity of environmental problems and the need to study them, not only thoroughly, but also very rapidly, in order to find a solution at Community level, have led the Commission to choose five priority measures to be started immediately:

1    the reduction of the concentration of the most dangerous pollutants in the air and water;

2    the reduction of pollution from the use of certain

commercial products and from substances arising out of
industrial production;

3     the improvement of knowledge of pollutants (their
origin, diffusion and effects) in order to reach these two goals;

4     the improvement of the open space and of the natural
environment;

5     the realisation of basic studies to a better knowledge,
identification and solution of the environmental problems
not touched by the points mentioned.

These measures should be backed up by an increasing participation of the Community in the work of international organisations
and by co-operation with other countries.

With regard to point 1, the reduction of the concentration of
the most dangerous pollutants in the air and water, the subjects of
study will be:

*for air*     − sulphur dioxide and particles in suspension
             − lead
             − photochemical reactions and nitrogen oxides
             − carbon monoxide
             − carcinogenic products (especially carcinogenic
               hydrocarbons)

*for water* − phosphates and nitrogenous derivatives
             − hydrocarbons and phenols
             − effluents of urban origin
             − micropollutants
             − thermal effects

For each of these substances or pollutants, taken separately or
combined, a common methodology must be established in order
to set basic levels for the Community.

As for water pollutants, the targets and criteria will be chosen
by taking into account the different uses of water (for drinking,
agricultural or industrial use). In a first phase, special attention will
be given to the harmonisation of targets and criteria for liquid
effluents, because of their great importance and effects on costs of

industrial and agricultural production.

In order to arrive at common action to reduce pollution in the Community, it is essential to use an approach and methods of assessment which are generally accepted. The following procedure should be envisaged:

a   assessment of targets allowing for the determination of the nature and the importance of harmful effects from pollutants on man and his environment;

b   harmonisation of methods of measurement and of interpretation of collected data;

c   determination of criteria or indicators; that is to say, the levels of concentration, exposition and absorption of pollutants corresponding to certain specific effects on man and his environment. In this context two classes of critera are to be distinguished:

— those referring to the effects of pollutants on human health,

— those referring to the effects on other organisms or on biological processes taken as reference targets for evaluating the alteration of the quality of natural resources;

d   adoption of minimum sanitary standards, based on these targets and criteria, and compulsory for the Community; and of environmental quality regulations, eventually even more rigid, on a regional or local level and which could differ from one region to another:

e   establishment of a common methodology for determining, on an appropriate regional, national or cummunity level, the emission standards called for by the above-mentioned regulations;

f   organisation of a community network for observation and monitoring of air and water quality and the establishment of appropriate measures to supervise emission standards;

g   periodic revision of criteria, indicators and regulations to take into consideration improvement of knowledge and scientific progress.

In carrying this out, the maximum use should be made of work done elsewhere in the member states, and by international organisations, in relation to human health and protection of the natural environment.

Point 2 of these priority measures deals with the reduction of pollution from the use of certain commercial products and from certain industrial and agricultural processes.

Pending the introduction of directly applicable Community regulations to support the general programme, the Commission thinks that it is necessary to:

accelerate the procedure of the 'general programme for the removal of technical barriers to trade' and finalise Community directives on this matter as rapidly as possible;

add to the list of products now contained in the general programme the following items: aircraft engines (noise, pollution); steam-driven locomotives and tractors; packaging; machines and equipment for the manufacture of pulp, paper and cardboard (water pollution, odour); machines and equipment for the preparation and working of leather and skins (water pollution, odour); machine-tools for working stone, ceramics, concrete, asbestos and other similar materials (air and water pollution).

The observation of regulations concerning the composition of certain commercial products, as well as the use of certain manfacturing procedures, will involve industry in important economic consequences which must be studied at Community level and, if necessary, on international level. In certain special cases of pollution abatement, considerable investment will be required by industry. It will be necessary to make sure that identical principles are applied in the assignment of additional expenditures in the member states of the Community.

If aid is necessary, as, for example, in the case of special situations of certain firms or under particular conditions of international competition, such aid should be harmonised and possibly granted at Community level.

As regards processes, the Commission intends to examine pollution problems in conjunction with interested parties, especially in the following:

the iron and steel industry (where the results of research on brown fumes, carried out as part of the Coal and Steel Community research programme, can be applied immediately) and in the metallurgical industry in general;
the paper and pulp industry (in close collaboration with OECD);
the chemical and petrochemical industry;
energy production.

The principle, according to which any new plant of a certain size should not only meet the emission standards referred to above, but should also use the most effective processes, techniques and equipment for reducing pollution, should be discussed with interested parties.

As for pollution caused by agriculture, it will be necessary to reduce substantially the use of certain persistent pesticides and insecticides and of certain fertilizers.

Point 3 of the priority measures is the improvement of knowledge on pollutants and the operation of a co-ordinated research programme.

The establishment of targets, criteria, and general and regional regulations of sanitary and environmental quality character requires a deep knowledge of polluting substances, their diffusion and effects on man and his environment. Further research will be essential to that end. New methods for the control of pollution must also be developed. The discovery of new products and less-polluting manufacturing processes require, in the light of costs involved, strong co-ordination on an international level. The Commission, in addition to the research projects that it suggests be carried out at the Joint Research Centre as part of its multi-annual research and training programme, and the anti-pollution projects that emerge from the work of the COST Working Party, will shortly put forward a co-ordinated programme of pollution research for the Community.

The measures (point 4) for improvement of open spaces and the natural environment are aimed at the conservation, improvement and management of a high-quality environment, and the development of communities in sparsely populated areas, in order to prevent or reduce high concentrations of population or activities in small areas.

The participation of the Community in existing or future national activities for regional planning is aimed at an equilibrated development of the regions and the preservation of those of particular interest to the community, eg coastal regions, town concentrations, developing agricultural zones. Special attention will be given to the problems of pollution in the Rhine River basin, the Mediterranean and the North Sea. For this purpose, close co-operation is envisaged between the Community and competent existing national and international bodies and organisations, especially with the International Commission for the Protection of the Rhine River against pollution.

As far as marine pollution is concerned, the Commission intends to start by studying the situation, the proposed solutions and recommendations (especially those on pollution by hydrocarbons, pesticides, detergents, heavy metals, urban and domestic waste, and dumping of industrial wastes). In the second stage, those organisations which are the most advanced in studying the specific pollution problems of the Mediterranean and the North Sea will be contacted to accelerate and complete these studies and recommendations. In the third stage, consultations will take place with the countries bordering these areas on practical action against the undesirable effects of such pollution, in order to restore the natural environment and preserve certain coastal regions as protected zones for tourism and recreation.

Finally, point 5 of the priority measures groups some specific studies which are necessary to complete the available data.

It is apparent that the powers available to the Community are not always consistent with the existing laws of the member states. If regulations are adopted too quickly (and this may result from the urgent need to protect human health and the environment), we may find we have set up barriers to trade, or that we have inadvertently distorted the conditions of economic competition. The qualitative improvement of living conditions through an attack on pollution is now a necessary and integrated aspect of economic development throughout the Community – a task assigned to the Community by Article 2 of the EEC Treaty.

This task must – in accordance moreover, with the case-law made by the Court of Justice – be interpreted harmoniously with current economic factors of which environmental problems are today undoubtedly a part. The Commission therefore feels, that when the Treaties do no expressly provide powers to act to this end, use should be made of Article 235 to implement a general action programme.

Now what will be the effects on UK standards policy of joining EEC?

Firstly, Great Britain will profit by the ECSC funds for research and investment in the coal and steel fields.

Secondly, Great Britain will have to comply with the rules of Chapter III of the EURATOM Treaty: to incorporate basic standards in its law, to send information on measurements of ambient radioactivity recorded in Great Britain, and to submit to the Commission plans for the discharge of radioactive waste.

Thirdly, Great Britain will have to comply with the directives already adopted on permissible noise level and motor-vehicle exhaust systems and pollution of the atmosphere by automotive petrol engines.

Fourthly, Great Britain will have to participate in the elaboration of other directives.

There are obligations deriving from the existing treaties. The general action programme I have described will be elaborated and decided on by the ten member states together. This programme has not yet been presented to the Council. It is under discussion with the national authorities. We are going to discuss it with the British authorities, and I wonder whether we have not started this discussion today.

To conclude: it came out very clearly from the discussion we had yesterday that there seems to be a double need:

a     for a forum discussion on the best ways to assess practical actions at national level;

b     for a European institute to decide and implement those measures should be taken at a wider, more international level, taking into consideration specific European interests.

We think that the enlarged European Community is particularly adapted to answer both needs.

## AN INDUSTRIAL VIEW OF INTERNATIONAL ENVIRONMENTAL PROBLEMS   *J. F. T. Langley*

As a British industrialist, I am happy to say that on international matters there is a very close identity of view between industry, as represented by the CBI, and government on the issues involved.

In contrast to some of our opposite numbers abroad, we have argued for a flexible approach to the fixing of standards. We believe that we should aim for international agreement on *objectives*, but we have misgivings about internationally agreed standards, except in special cases. For the most part such cases would be those in which pollution is not solely an internal matter, but is exportable. Obvious examples are pollution of the Rhine, the Mediterranean, the Baltic and the North Sea. Our reasons for being sceptical of international standards in general are these:

It is argued that uniform standards across the world would result in a reduction of pollution. This presupposes that the best national practices would be adopted. The reverse is more likely to happen; a levelling down rather than a levelling up which would improve nothing. Uniform standards would require an elaborate system of monitoring, inspection and enforcement.

Secondly, uniform standards would have no regard for the natural capacity of the environment to absorb and disperse pollutants. This would in many cases result in a wasteful use of scarce resources which could have been better employed.

Thirdly, the mind boggles at the prospect of negotiating uniform standards. The arguments would be interminable, the numbers of 'exceptional cases' would be astronomical, and as a result, progress in areas where solutions are comparatively straight forward, would be held up. One can visualise a situation in which nothing gets done because everything cannot be done.

Fourthly, there is danger of widening the already alarming gap between the developed and the less developed countries. This is something I have referred to elsewhere under the heading of non-tariff barriers, Briefly, the problem is that less developed countries may regard any attempt to impose uniform standards as a deliberate measure to retard their economic growth. By definition, the less developed countries enjoy conditions in which their environment still has considerable capacity safely to dilute or disperse pollutants.

There is one argument frequently advanced in favour of inter-nationally uniform standards which I would like to explore. This is the argument that if the national standards of one country are at odds with those of another, a degree of unfair industrial competition will exist, the more conscientious companies being at a disadvantage compared with those who neglect their environmental responsibilities. The argument is superficially seductive but, in the view of the CBI, not well founded. Few of the burdens on industry are uniform. Transport costs, labour costs, taxation systems, raw material availability — all vary widely both nationally and regionally. There seems little object in singling out environmental pollution as a special case. There is as yet no means of harmonising the weather, but as far as I know no-one has suggested that in the interests of equalising competition the Italians should be required to grow their tomatoes under glass.

The objective is to check and reduce the pollution of the environment. To achieve this we must use the methods which are the most effective and the most appropriate in a given set of circumstances. Not to utilise the environment's considerable capacity to absorb pollutants in a misguided attempt at international uniformity would constitute a wasteful use of scarce resources and impede progress towards our goal. Certainly comparisons of national practices with regard to emission standards will be valuable, but it will only confuse the issue if the control of pollution is brought into the arena of theoretical trade and economic arguments relating to competitiveness.

For these reasons we believe that, while there may be some cases where uniform international standards are appropriate, these will be relatively few and that as a general rule the concept of using emission standards as a means of levelling competition is unsound. There seem to me to be two aspects of the problem of the repercussions on international trade of standards policy: the effect of the standards policy of one industrialised country upon another, and the effect of the standards policies of industrialised countries upon the developing countries, and vice-versa. Of these two aspects the second seems to me the most important.

As regards the industrialised countries, it seems to me that all are faced with broadly similar pollution problems, and all are beginning to think along broadly similar lines and are likely to come up with broadly similar solutions. I would not have thought that differences of pollution standards as between one industrialised country and another, taken over a period of time, would be such as to cause serious distortion of trade or movement of capital. There is, however, one aspect which may give rise to difficulty. This is the question of the method adopted for payment for pollution control. If, for example, Country A adopts the principle of building the cost of pollution control into the price of the product and

Country B elects to subsidise the cost of pollution control heavily
out of central taxation, firms in Country A could clearly be placed
at a serious disadvantage. It might become necessary to declare
Country B's policy an unfair trading practice, in which case it
would be proscribed under the appropriate trade treaty, EFTA,
EEC or GATT. There are plenty of precedents for international
action of this sort; anti-dumping legislation and export subsidies
for example; but I have to add in parenthesis that it is somewhat
easier to make rules under trade treaties than it is to enforce them.

The greater problem seems to me to lie between the industrialised countries and the less developed countries. If one accepts, as
I think I do, that most forms of pollution stem from industrialisation,
then by definition the less developed countries are less industrially
polluted. That they have their own particular sorts of pollution,
such as shanty towns, impoverishment of the land, inadequate or
non-existent sewerage, is not to be denied, but this is not really
what we are talking about.

What we are talking about is the pollution criteria which we
should apply to the industrial processes of the developing countries.
Most of these countries have not reached critical pollution levels.
They have thus a great opportunity to avoid the mistakes made in
the past. It is in our interests to offer wise and generous guidance
to help them achieve this. These countries need modern technology
if they are to make economic progress. We must remember that
because of their economic circumstances the preservation of the
environment is not necessarily one of their highest priorities. The
quantity of life to them is still more important than the quality. It
is difficult to deny them the right to decide what levels of pollution
they are prepared to tolerate in return for faster economic growth.

There are, however, ways in which we can help them to take the
right course for the future. Where industrial plant is manufactured
for them in the developed countries, we must try to ensure that
clean technology is used and that adequate pollution control devices are built in, even though the local pollution standards may be

low or non-existent. If we decide to invest in these countries, we are entitled to use to our advantage the ability of their environment safely to absorb a degree of pollution, but we must take care not to do this to the extent of building up trouble for future generations.

It may be that, because of their late entry upon the industrial scene and the availability of new and improved pollution control devices, they will find it unnecessary to impose the stringent pollution standards which are required in the countries whose industries are based on older technologies and who face a backlog of environmental neglect. If this seems to give the developing countries a competitive advantage, we must accept this with generosity. Any attempt to impose unnecessarily strict pollution standards upon them or to penalise their exports will be seen as an attempt to erect non-tariff barriers and to stifle their economic growth. This would be shortsighted in the extreme. Although it may not be relevant to this discussion, I cannot help observing that the ever-widening gap between the haves and the have-nots is just as great a problem as environmental pollution, and any measures which might have the effect of impeding the closing of this gap must be firmly resisted even at considerable short-term cost to the developed countries.

I would in conclusion mention two anxieties in my mind. The first is the proliferation of international organisations which are active in matters relating to the environment. In Europe alone there are no less than nine, which have environmental committees or commissions or panels or working parties or study groups or round tables. You name it; they have it. They are:

United Nations Economic Commission for Europe
European Economic Community
Union des Industries de la Communaute Europeenne
Council of European Industrial Federations
Organisation for Economic Co-operation and Development
Business and Industrial Advisory Committee to OECD

        International Chamber of Commerce
        North Atlantic Treaty Organisation
        Council of Europe
    To a varying extent the CBI has contact with all these organisations.
It could, I suppose, be argued that it is highly encouraging that they
should all be involving themselves in one of the great questions of
the century; but one cannot help feeling that there is an element of
'climbing on the bandwagon', that the overlapping and waste of resources must be colossal, that such proliferation will make concerted
action more difficult and that some sort of rationalisation must
take place. It will not be easy, because the environment is now the
'in' thing. There is, though, a great danger that the man on the
Clapham bus, who is just becoming aware of the problem and
whose co-operation we must have, will become bored by the vocifer-
ous but apparently unco-ordinated activities of all these organisations. His natural reaction will be — 'if they can't agree amongst
themselves, why should I worry?'
    Finally, and in one sentence, the population explosion. This
problem baffles me completely, and yet I am certain we are
approaching the crunch, that something will have to be done, and
that it will have to be done certainly within my lifetime, in other
words, the next twenty years. My mind recoils before the possibility of euthanasia, of families by licence, of compulsory
sterilisation. To minds brought up in our liberal traditions, these
thoughts are chilling. Yet there is little public debate — perhaps
because the implications *are* so chilling. Few are prepared to face
them. There have been many gloomy forebodings about what may
happen in twenty, fifty or one hundred years, and much wringing
of hands, but so far little attempt to suggest solutions. The problem must, I believe, be brought into international debate in
practical rather than prophetic terms. In recent years we seem to
have made some progress in limiting the spread of nuclear weapons;
the population problem is just as menacing and far more difficult.

## DISCUSSION
Some of those present expressed doubts about the contention of Mr Arculus and Mr Langley that it was unnecessary to set international standards for the sake of 'fairness' in industrial competition, and that national governments could be left to determine their national standards except where pollution crossed national frontiers or where a diversity of standards for polluting products would be an obstacle to trade. It was argued, for example, that unless international standards were set more widely, international companies would tend to locate their factories where control of pollution was least exacting. Professor Beckerman replied that this would imply one of two things. Either the circumstances in the country chosen would be such that the value of the presence of the factory exceeded the disbenefit of the pollution it caused, in which case the government of the country concerned had been right to attract it there; or the disbenefit would exceed the benefit, in which case the country concerned would be better off without the factory. It was open to governments to bring about the result they desired by the use of fiscal measures of the kind he had suggested. These could take account of all relevant factors, including, for example, the advantages of attracting foreign capital. The benefits might be such that a polluting industry was not taxed at all: it might even be subsidised.

Other speakers supported the arguments Mr Arculus and Mr Langley had developed. Dr Holdgate gave as an example of a risk of 'levelling down' the fact that if the United Kingdom were obliged to adopt the EEC standard of biodegradability for detergents, foaming would reappear in rivers in the United Kingdom because present UK standards were higher. Mr Price, however, said that he could think at once of three fields in which 'levelling up' was a more probable result of international standards; namely, emissions of $SO_2$, measures to make cars safer, and noise from vehicles. It had been his experience in the OECD Transport Committee that governments found that problems they had previously thought

intractable were in fact being tackled successfully by other governments. More generally, it was, he suggested, significant that a
meeting of fewer than ten countries could deal with three-quarters
of the world's industrial effort.

Several speakers suggested that the international regulation of
pollutants that crossed frontiers and of 'traded pollutants', which
was generally agreed to be indispensable, would prove more complicated and exacting than was sometimes supposed and would
react with other economic discussions. Dr MacDonald said that his
government was conducting regular bilateral discussions with the
government of Japan on licensing of polluting products (especially
vehicles) and on the development of the market for pollution control equipment, in the context of wider issues of the effects of
internal economic policies on the health of international trade.
Practical and detailed discussions, which it was hoped would shortly
lead to the conclusion of a treaty or an executive agreement, had
been needed to reconcile the views of the United States and
Canadian governments on the protection of the Great Lakes.
Bilateral negotiations with Mexico had not proceeded far, but one
serious issue had already been raised. From 1973, unless Mexico
provided a non-leaded petrol, there would have to be signs on the
border saying 'If your car is a '73 model or later, turn back'. Since
United States' tourism is Mexico's second largest industry, Mexico
seemed likely soon to be on its way to providing non-leaded petrol.
Mr Price suggested that the need to establish common standards
and codes of practice to protect the North Sea and the Rhine
would ultimately have far-reaching consequences. Again, the United
States' interest in the 91 octane car would certainly be of considerable interest to the European producers of small highly-rated
engines working at high compression ratios. There could not fail
to be reactions between the policies of different countries, whether
or not formal machinery was set up in the fields in question. The
benefits of replacing coal by other fuels might be much smaller
than the indirect social costs, if the result were the decline of the

mining industry, with the creation of unemployment and abandoning of townships, and a change in the whole market situation for
oil. The ramifications through a community's patterns of settlement
and employment could be colossal. In Geneva recently a Canadian
delegate said, 'The direct cost of pollution control for almost all
industries is very little more than an additional one per cent on their
present expenditure', and someone else said, 'Ah, yes, but on the
other hand the cost to the economy of Bolivia if the whole world
ceased to put lead into petrol could be catastrophic because of the
importance of lead exports to Bolivia'. Almost every major
pollution control scheme could involve widely dispersed national
and even international consequences. Dr Holdgate added that
where pollutants crossed frontiers there would be formidable problems about where the costs of abatement or of failure to abate
should fall. Such problems would arise, for example, if it were
established, as the Swedish government believed it would be, that
forestry and fisheries in Sweden and Norway were being seriously
harmed by acidification origination in other countries.

Finally, stress was laid on the importance of the proper international organisation and use of research. Dr Pochin suggested that
international recommendations could be applied to problems of
atmospheric contamination in a way that they have been developed
successfully in regard to ionising radiation. He believed that the
situations were comparable, since ideally it was the function of a
body like the International Commission on Radiological Protection
to estimate and assert the degree of risk or of safety for any given
practice or level of exposure, and not to make laws which are
binding upon different countries. Any country must be in a
position to say that it feels obliged to accept a higher risk from a
given procedure or occupation than is recommended as suitable by
an International Commission. The value of a central and authoritative scientific body of this sort was to assert as quantitatively as
as possible the degree of safety involved in various levels of
exposure and to recommend the procedures that it regards as

optimal, and not to legislate explicitly on national practice. Dr Price said that communication was being handicapped by defects in organisation, and especially overlapping between international organisations, and between them and national bodies. Vast international research organisations were to be avoided: research was usually better organised nationally. The right course was to use the various national organisations to develop national scientific views and then to compare these views in an international forum. Differences that emerged at that stage might be important pointers towards further research and action.

Notes to this chapter are on page 198

# 6: Summing Up

Like all seminars which cover a wide field, summing-up becomes an exercise in selection. I propose to start with the economic framework because the one thing that became more and more clear to me as we proceeded was that in the long term the economic issue is not the most important of the many that we discussed. There are other aspects of the problem of the environment which clearly affect us more. In his very forceful presentation, Beckerman made it quite plain that pollution is not something which one should expect to be stopped altogether, but something which has to be reduced to tolerable levels. The optimum point of reduction 'is where the social costs of further abatement would exceed the social costs . . . of the remaining pollution. This is the optimum level of pollution, and it is quite distinct from the question of who should bear the social costs of pollution at the optimum. The latter issue is a matter of income distribution and equity, and is nothing to do with the question of what is optimum output'.

When we turned to the international aspects of the problem, it became plain that we could not expect everybody to behave in the same way. There would be too many dislocations in international relations and in international trade if there were too rapid an attempt to conform to common standards. But, from the point of view of the economist, if we assume that countries like India or Africa or Brazil go on 'polluting' now more than do others, they

will, in effect, merely be adding to their future problems. If the
right measures are not taken now to protect the environment, if
the resources for their solution are unavailable now, they will have
to be found later. But only political trouble can follow if too
forceful an effort is made to deal with environmental problems
now. That is one general thought which I certainly gained from
the discussion.

Another which I gained in the same context was considered this
afternoon. If our national environmental standards became too
rigid, or if we decided to impose uniform international standards
– something to which I think everybody at this symposium is
opposed – we would definitely run into difficulties. There is,
however, no need to do this. What we really want to do is to make
certain that we have all got the right environmental objectives, the
right goals. We do not want to impose on all people standards which
are applicable only in particular circumstances, and which may be
unnecessary in others. That way would lead to unfair international
competition. It could certainly induce underdeveloped countries
to hold back. We are talking about action to protect the environment in advanced democratic societies. The imposition of our own
standards in developing countries could lead to reaction – not only
in the national sphere but also in international debate. If we do not
bear in mind the difficulties, we shall certainly handicap discussion
in the international forum.

In the final analysis, we end up with the problem which was put
to us at our first session – about the nature of environmental
standards. Who sets a standard? What standards? One thing is
certain. We need more information. We need more environmental
research in industry. This morning's discussion made us realise that
we need to be made aware of the problems. It is not enough that
some of us are aware of the problems. What matters is that the
country at large has got to become aware of them. Something like
a *Torrey Canyon*, a typhoid disaster, something of that sort seems
to be needed in order to bring matters of this kind into the public

conscience, so that political action can follow. And when action is taken, there has got to be somebody who knows what is wrong, who has enquired thoroughly into the matter, and is ready to set the standards. In the case of radioactive hazards, there is international agreement. But at the present moment I do not know whether we have really faced the problem of who settles the kind of disputes that occur between the scientists who set the standards. We have evaded that issue in this seminar. Unless he has managed to sort the matter out, I believe that at this moment Professor Lawther has some major differences with one or two of his opposite numbers in the United States. Unless the journal *Science* gives an incorrect picture of what goes on in the United States, there are also disputes within that country.

How are we going to settle these things? Unless we do find a means whereby they can be settled, then there will be disagreement about standards, and if the disagreements cannot be settled nationally, they certainly won't be settled internationally. For that reason, I would wish to endorse Gordon Macdonald's plea about the necessity to get international assessments done in a way which is sensible, and in a way in which responsible scientists can speak properly to those who are responsible for taking political decisions, so that the politicians themselves are led to wide decisions and are not misled into needless overaction. I'm absolutely certain that we want a somewhat better organisation than we now have. I was glad to hear from Mr Langley that industry is partaking fully in discussions with government about various agreements. That was a good general statement. But I know that major disagreements do occur, that industry has not always been ready to accept the views of government, and that government has not been ready to accept the views of industry, and where the compromises which may have had to be made may have been all right nationally, but not necessarily internationally.

In the setting of standards, we are always dealing with a balance of risk. Standards constitute practical problems, problems of applied

science. The cyclamates story was brought up. Cyclamates produced
tumour in the bladder of some rates or mice or whatever the animals
were which were tested. But do we really know whether the substance can also induce bladder cancers in human beings? And is the
frequency of these tumours in human beings of such consequence,
in relation to all other tumours which human beings may get from
causes that have not yet been identified, to justify the action that
was taken?

I sometimes wonder whether we are not running into the danger
in the environmental field of having it dealt with by an organisation
like the US Pure Food and Drugs Administration which deals with
all new drugs in the United States. The FDA is always up against
the job of proving a negative. So? I understand that *no new drugs
have been passed in the last two years*. This is no light matter. I
doubt, for example, whether the 'Pill' would pass the FDA today,
as it did some years ago. It is one of the few effective measures we
have for restraining the growth of population. Yet the various
environmental organisations which already exist in the United
States, in order ostensibly to protect the public — leave alone the
new ones about which we were told by Gordon MacDonald —
could get us into trouble if we do not go about the job of securing
scientific agreement about risks in the most cautious way possible.
We need to be farsighted when judging of a balance of risk. Human
resources are limited; human population is growing at a far more
rapid rate than that at which resources can be deployed where they
are needed.

Yet clearly the environment is a very important thing so far as
the future is concerned. I was fascinated by Gordon MacDonald's
statement about what it would cost to abate pollution in the
United States over the next five years; that it amounts to about
two per cent of the USA GNP. Two per cent of its GNP is a
pretty considerable figure. It adds up to something like $20 billion.
That is just about a tenth of what the world is spending at the
present moment in a year on military preparations. But it is more

than all technical aid and credits and loans to the developing
countries. I would like to know — and this is a question which
needs to be asked — whether the problem which we have been
discussing for the past two days merits an expenditure of $20
billion a year in the United States. From the point of view of
doing good for tomorrow, shouldn't those resources have been
channelled to some other purpose — say, aid? Who is to
answer?

This is the question of priorities which Chilver raised when
we were discussing the matter in a national context. Priorities
are of the essence of politics — politics is about transitional
problems, problems of dislocation. We have got to view our environmental problems, not only in a national, but also in an international context. We have held this seminar at a very opportune
moment. To the best of my knowledge, this is the first time in
the history of government where a major issue, one which
affects both the history and the future of humanity as a whole,
has been dealt with by scientists from the outset with politicians.
I know of no other case. I believe that the kind of discussion
that we have had, and the discussions which are taking place in
the United Nations and in the EEC, as well as binationally, are
all illustrative of the fact that informed scientific opinion can
now be brought to bear on major political action where the
politician, unaided, would be helpless. I am indeed happy that
we have had the opportunity of this seminar for discussing a
major problem at a formative stage. On behalf of the University,
may I thank all of you who have attended, and particularly our
visitors from abroad.

# List of Abbreviations

COST      Committee for Overseas Science and Technology
EAGGF     European Agricultural Guidance and Guarantee Fund
ECE       Export Council for Europe
ECSC      European Coal and Steel Community
EEC       European Economic Community
EPA       Environmental Protection Agency
ESC       Economic and Social Council
EURATOM   European.Atomic Energy Community
FAO       Food and Agriculture Organisation
FDA       Food and Drug Administration (USA)
GATT      General Agreement on Tariffs and Trade
IAEA      International Atomic Energy Agency
ICAO      International Civil Aviation Organisation
ICRP      International Commission on Radiological Protection
ICSU      International Council of Scientific Unions
IMCO      Intergovernmental Maritime Consultative
          Organisation (USA)
ISO       International Organisation for Standardisation
OECD      Organisation for Economic Co-operation and
          Development

| UNCTAD | United Nations Conference on Trade and Development |
| UNIDO | United Nations Industrial Development Organisation |
| UNSCEAR | United Nations Scientific Committee on the Effects of Atomic Radiation |
| WHO | World Health Organisation |
| WMO | World Meteorological Organisation |

# Notes and References

## 2 THE SCIENTIFIC INPUT

1   Stalker, W. W. et al. 'Sampling station and time requirements for urban
    air pollution surveys' *J. Air Poll. Cont. Ass.* (1962) Part 3, 170 and
    Part 4, 361
2   Davies, T. D. Unpublished research (1970)
3   Junge, C. E. *Air Chemistry and Radioactivity* (1963)
4   Davies, T. D. Unpublished PhD thesis, University of Sheffield (1972)
5   Reed, L. E. and Barrett, C. F. 'Air Pollution from road traffic in
    Archway Road, London' *Int. J. Air Wat. Poll.* 9 (1965)
6   Martin, A. and Barber, F. 'Some measurements of loss of atmospheric
    $SO_2$ near foliage', *Atmospheric Environment,* 5 (1971) 425
7   Garnett, A. Records of Air Pollution Research Unit, University of
    Sheffield
8   Harrington, J. B. et al 'High efficiency pollen samples for use in clinical
    allergy' *J. Allergy,* 30 (1959) 357
9   Hage, K. D. et al. 'On horizontal flat-plate sampling of solid particles
    in the atmosphere' *AMA Arch. Ind. Health,* 21 (1960) 124
10  Martin, A. and Barber, F. 'Control of daily $SO_2$ instruments to minimise
    possible errors', *Atmospheric Environment,* 5 (1971) 425
11  Danckwerts, P. V. *Gas-Liquid Reactions* (1970), 145; Liss, P. S. 'The
    Exchange of Gases across the Air-Sea Interface' Meteorological Research
    Committee Paper No 302 (1971)
12  Bolin, B. 'On the Exchange of Carbon Dioxide between the Atmosphere
    and the Sea', *Tellus,* 12 (1960), 274-81; Liss, P. S. Processes of gas
    exchange across an air-water interface, *Deep-Sea Research,* 20 (1973),
    221-238

*195*

13    Craig, H. 'The Natural Distribution of Radiocarbon and the Exchange
      Time of Carbon Dioxide between Atmosphere and Sea', *Tellus*, 9
      (1957) 1-17
14    Munn, R. E. and Bolin, B. 'Global Air Pollution – Meteorological
      Aspects', *Atmospheric Environment*, 5 (1971) 363-402
15    Liss, P. S. 'Exchange of $SO_2$ between the Atmosphere and Natural
      Waters', *Nature*, 233 (1971), 327-9
16    Brimblecombe, P. and Spedding, D. J. Rate of Solution of Gaseous
      Sulphur Dioxide at Atmospheric Concentrations', *Nature*, 236 (1972),
      225
17    Junge, C. E. *Air Chemistry and Radioactivity*, 3 (1963)
18    Bien, G. S. Contois, D. E. and Thomas, W. H. 'The removal of soluble
      silica from fresh water entering the sea', *Geochim Cosmochim. Acta*, 14
      (1958), 35-54
19    Liss, P. S. and Spencer, C. P. 'Abiological processes in the removal of
      silicate from sea water', *Geochim. Cosmochim. Acta*. 34 (1970) 1073-88
20    Wollast, R. and de Broeu, F. 'Study of behaviour of dissolved silica in the
      estuary of the Scheldt', *Geochim. Cosmochim. Acta*, 35 (1971) 613-20
21    Liss, P. S. and Pointon, M. J. 'Removal of Dissolved Boron and Silicon
      during Estuarine Mixing of Sea and River Waters', *Geochim. Cosmochim.
      Acta*, 37 (1973) 1493-98
22    Butler, E. I. and Tibbitts, S. 'Chemical Survey of the Tamar Estuary',
      *J. Mar. Biol. Assoc. UK*. (1972)
23    Ryther, J. H. and Dunstan, W. M. 'Nitrogen, Phosphorus and Eutrophi-
      cation in the Coastal Marine Environment', *Science*, 171 (1971) 1008-13


## 3  THE ECONOMIC AND SOCIAL INPUTS
1    'Sweden puts Pollution in its place', *Le Monde Weekly* (27 May 1971);
     *see also* Pavitt, Keith, 'A European View of the ' Environmental Crisis" '.
     lecture (17 March 1971) in series 'Rescuing Man's Environment'
     sponsored by the Council of Environmental Studies, Princeton
     University; and 'Pollution Control', *Financial Times* (11 August 1971),
     for information about the reduction of mercury pollution in the Kema
     Nord chlorine plant in Sweden
2    See 106th Annual Report on Alkali, Etc Works 1969 (1970)
3    In Britain, Mr Fred Lester, the Pollution Control Officer of the Trent

River Authority, was probably expressing the view found among nearly all officials concerned with the control of water pollution, when he opposed the suggestion, recently put forward by the Ramblers' Association, that a pollution tax should be introduced. He said it would be better to make offending industries and local councils spend more on effluent treatment plant; reported in the *Lincolnshire Echo* (5 August 1971)

4 Several examples are reported in the latest annual report of the President's Council on Environmental Quality. *See also* note 21

5 'Pollute and Pay Study in US', *The Guardian* (14 July 1971). In the same vein, a recent article in *Business Week* states that: 'In one form or another, effluent charges look like an idea whose time has come. Environmentalists, who once opposed the scheme as a 'licence to pollute', now solidly back the idea.' *See* note 21

6 Kneese, Allen 'The Economics of Environmental Pollution in the United States', extract from a paper prepared for the Atlantic Council, (December 1970).

7 'Industry Action to Combat Pollution', *Harvard Business Review*, (September - October 1966).

8 'A Study of Pollution – Air'. A Staff Report to the Committee on Public Works, US Senate (Washington, Government Printing Office, September 1963).

9 'The Cost of Clean Air', First Report of the Secretary of Health, Education and Welfare to the Congress of the US, in Compliance with the P.L. 90 - 148. The Air Quality Act of 1967

10 US News and World Report, (August 1970).

11 Gerhard, P. 'Incentives to Air Pollution Control' *Law and Contemporary Problems* Vol 33 No 2 (1968).

12 Leontief, W. 'Environmental Repercussions and the Economic Structure – an Input-Output Approach', *Review of Economics and Statistics* (August 1970)

13 'Japan Fights Environmental Pollution', *Fuji Bank Bulletin,* (March 1971).

14 See article by Reginald Cudlip, Director of the Anglo-Japanese Economic Institute, *The Financial Times* (5 July 1971). Some interesting details on the way some of the expenditures are to be allocated in Tokyo are given in note 22

15    'Taken for Granted', (Jeger Report) Report of the Working Party on
      Sewage Disposal (1970)
16    Mr Peter Walker interview in *The Evening Standard* and in speech to a
      constituency meeting in Droitwich, reported in the *Birmingham Post*,
      (3 September 1971).
17    105th Annual Report on Alkali, Etc. Works 1968 (1969)
18    This includes a generous allowance for the costs of water disposal, in
      the light of estimates attributed in *The Times*, (9 September 1971) to
      Mr F Flintoff, an engineering consultant.
19    'The Progress and Effects of Smoke Control in London' GLC Research
      and Intelligence Unit, (February 1970)
20    'Growing Industrial Expenditures for Pollution Control', *The Conference
      Board Record, Montreal,* Vol VIII No 2, (February, 1970)
21    'Paying for Pollution by the Pound' *Business Week,* (4 September 1961)
22    'Paying for Pollution'. Bureau of General Affairs, Tokyo Metropolitan
      Government, (March 1971).
23    See 2nd Annual Report of the Council of Environmental Quality
      (August 1971) 120-1 for references and summary

## 4 GOVERNMENT PROCESSES IN DETERMINING AND APPLYING CONTROLS

Dr Holdgate's paper at the Seminar was supported by two annexes. One was
an extract from the Report of the Third Session of the Preparatory Committee for the United Nations Conference on the Human Environment and set
out a series of definitions which explain the terms used in Dr Holdgate's
paper is reprinted below, but in view of the developments since the seminar,
the supporting material has been omitted. The second annexe circulated with
Dr Holdgate's paper of the Seminar was a position paper on standards submitted by the United Kingdom government to the Secretariat preparing for
the Stockholm Conference, and this was subsequently circulated with other
official British papers to the participants in the Stockholm Conference
itself. This paper has not been reprinted here, but a summary of its contents
is set out below.

Standards— appendix to the paper by M. W. Holdgate
**PART I — Terminology**

## A – BASIC TERMINOLOGY

*1. Exposure* – the amount of a particular physical or chemical agent that reaches the target.

*2. Risk* – the expected frequency of undesirable effects arising from a given exposure to a pollutant.

*3. Target (or receptor)* – the organism, population or resource to be protected from specified risks.

*B – CRITERIA* – the quantitative relations between the exposure to a pollutant and the risk or magnitude of an undesirable effect under specified circumstances defined by environmental variables and target variables.

## C – STANDARDS

*1. Primary protection standard* – an accepted maximum level of a pollutant (or its indicator) in the target or some part thereof, or an accepted maximum intake of a pollutant into the target under specified circumstances.

*2. Derived working levels* – maximum acceptable levels of pollutants in specified media other than the target designed to ensure that under specified circumstances a primary protection standard is not exceeded.

*3.* Derived working levels are known by a variety of names, including *environmental or ambient quality standards, maximum permissible limits and maximum allowable concentrations.* When derived working levels apply to products such as food or detergents, they may be known as *product standards.*

The maximum acceptable release of a pollutant from a given source to a specified medium under specified circumstances may be termed a *discharge* (or *effluent* or *emission*) *standard* or a *release limit.*

In order to meet such discharge standards or release limits, it may be necessary to set various types of *technological standards* or *codes of practice* concerned with the performance and design of those technologies or operations leading to the release of pollutants.

*4. Action level* – the level of a pollutant at which specified emergency countermeasures such as the seizure and destruction of contaminated materials, evacuation of the local population or closing down of the sources of pollution are to be taken.

## PART II – International Standards for Pollution Control

Summary of basic paper submitted by the United Kingdom to the UN Conference on the Human Environment

1. There are at least four definable types of pollution control standards: product standards, design standards, emission standards and environmental quality standards.
2. Differing national product and design standards can lead to the creation of non-tariff barriers.
3. Emission standards for the discharge of industrial effluent should be related to local conditions. Uniform international emission standards are undesirable, and would not equalise competition.
4. Evironmental quality standards based on emission standards, which in turn are related to local conditions, may provide an acceptable way of controlling certain forms of pollution,
5. International action should focus on areas of common concern with a view to improving the environment and avoiding unrealistically high or low standards. More scientific and economic information is needed.
6. There is a need to harmonise national product and design standards and avoid internationally uniform emission standards. National standards of emission control based on environmental quality will generally provide the best solution – subject to international scrutiny.

## 5 INTERNATIONAL PROCESSES

1    In his George Davis Medal 1969 lecture, 'Cleaning the Air', (Manchester 1970), Mr F E Ireland stated that: 'Preventing pollution is an international problem, for no country can afford to risk its international trade by progressing at a much faster pace than its rivals and thereby making its products uncompetitive'. (I hope that Mr Ireland will accept my assurances that the main reason I quote him again is that I tend to read what he writes with great respect and attention).
2    See Christy, F. and Scott, A. D. 'The Common Wealth of Ocean Fisheries' (Resources for the Future)

# Index